PRACTICING THE PRESENCE OF GOD

PRACTICING THE
PRESENCE OF GOD

A Modernized Christian Classic

by Brother Lawrence

Translation by Robert J. Edmonson, CJ
Introduction and Notes by Tony Jones

PARACLETE PRESS
Brewster, Massachusetts

Practicing the Presence of God

2009   Second Printing
2007   First Printing

Copyright © 2007 by The Community of Jesus, Inc.

Notes and Introduction copyright © 2007 by Tony Jones

ISBN: 978-1-55725-465-8

Library of Congress Cataloging-in-Publication Data

Lawrence, of the Resurrection, Brother, 1611–1691.
  [Pratique de la présence de Dieu. English]
  Practicing the presence of God : a modernized Christian classic / by
Brother Lawrence ; translation by Robert J. Edmonson ; introduction and
notes by Tony Jones.
      p. cm.
  Originally published: The practice of the presence of God. 1895.
With new introd. and notes.
  ISBN-13: 978-1-55725-465-8
  1. Christian life--Catholic authors. I. Edmonson, Robert J. II.
Jones, Tony, 1968- III. Title.
  BX2350.3.L3813 2007
  248.4'82--dc22   2007025372

10 9 8 7 6 5 4 3 2

Published by Paraclete Press

Brewster, Massachusetts

www.paracletepress.com

Printed in the United States of America

Contents

Translator's Note

Before I set out to translate the book you are about to read, I had an image of Brother Lawrence as a jolly monk who took pleasure in cleaning pots and cooking. What could he have to say to me?

As I began to read the sections of the book in which others wrote about Brother Lawrence, I felt a growing awareness that this humble lay brother led a life that does, indeed, have much to say to me, and when I read his own writings, I was struck by the depth of his love for God and his life lived in obedience, humility, and concern for others. Then I understood why I was translating this book: it was because I so needed to hear what it has to say. Session after session in front of the typewriter brought deeper and deeper conviction of who I am, and greater and greater hope for what God can do in a life wholly given to Him.

It is my prayer that you will also be blessed by this book, and that as you follow the example of Brother Lawrence, you, too, will be filled with the presence of God.

ROBERT J. EDMONSON

Introduction by Tony Jones

"Pray without ceasing."

When the apostle Paul first wrote these words to the church he had planted in Thessalonica, he may have thought that it was entirely natural for a person to pray continually. Maybe that was his experience.

But since those words were penned, Christians have struggled with how to apply them to their own lives. *Paul was exaggerating, right?,* we wonder, *for surely he didn't mean that literally! It's just not possible to pray without ceasing.*

So, for two millennia, saints and those of us who are not-quite-saints have endeavored to live a life that in some way aspires toward Paul's vision of ceaseless prayer.

In the history of our faith, it may be that no one has exemplified a life of continual prayer—and taught others about it—better than a humble monk who lived in seventeenth-century France. Brother Lawrence was not a saint, and he's never been made a saint. He wasn't even a priest. Instead, he was a simple man who committed his life to living every waking moment in the presence of God.

I

His words—simple like the man himself—have with-stood four centuries. We live in a much different time than Lawrence, a time of mobile phones and Internet access and twenty-four hour news, but his little book may be more popular today than ever before. Indeed, maybe it's because the world is so un-simple now that Brother Lawrence's words endure.

The Man and His Time

The seventeenth century was a time of transition, especially in France. In Europe, the Protestant Reformation, begun by Martin Luther, John Calvin, and others, was only one hundred years old, the printing press only two hundred. When Brother Lawrence was just nine years old, the persecuted Pilgrims boarded the Mayflower and set off to find religious freedom on a new continent. Many people must have felt that the long-standing religious landscape was shifting beneath their very feet. Across Europe, other sweeping changes were initiated by geniuses such as Galileo Galilei, Rene Descartes, Blaise Pascal, and Isaac Newton, men who birthed modern science and philosophy.

Meanwhile, France was enjoying its preeminence in the world. Louis XIV (a.k.a., Louis the Great, "The Sun King") reigned from 1643 until 1715. He saw the Thirty Years War to a close in 1648 and fought several other wars during his tenure as king, all of which solidified France's political and cultural clout across Europe, and established the French presence in the colonization of the Americas.

Into this world, Nicholas Herman was born in 1611. A peasant, he joined the army as a footman for the nobility and was thus guaranteed meals and a small salary. But at age eighteen, he saw a vision that altered the course of his life: looking at a dormant tree in the winter, he recognized that he, too, felt completely barren. However, he knew that the tree would come back to life in the spring, and Nicholas felt that God was about to bring him new life as well.

Circumstances demanded that he continue his service in the army for six more years, after which he arrived at the doorstep of the Carmelite monastery in Paris. The Carmelite Order had been founded in the twelfth century on Mt. Carmel in Israel, with an emphasis on the practice of contemplative prayer. But the order had become lax and political over the centuries, until St. Teresa of Avila and St. John of the Cross led a reform movement in the sixteenth century. They founded the Discalced ("without shoes") Carmelites, and it was this order of Carmelites that Nicholas Herman joined.

Lacking the education necessary to become a priest, Nicholas was given the name Brother Lawrence of the Resurrection and put to work doing the menial tasks of the uneducated brothers. He spent the majority of the next five decades working in the kitchen until he became too old and infirm for that and was reassigned to making sandals. Brother Lawrence died on February 12, 1691.

At first glance, his was the seemingly trivial life of a peasant monk who spent fifty-plus years working in the kitchen and the shoe shop. But what compelled Brother

Lawrence during his decades of monastic life was basically this: How can one be in a spirit of prayer, even while peeling potatoes? That is, how can a person commune with God, even while performing the most mundane tasks?

His answer: practice—more specifically, the practice of the presence of God.

In the following pages, you will read the thoughts of a man whose commitment to God is breathtaking and beautiful. Brother Lawrence made a habit of thinking about God in all things, drawing near to God at all times. Indeed, he was so disciplined in his ceaseless recollection of the Lord that it became habitual for him. It became a way of life.

The Book You Hold in Your Hands

This little book is a collection, really. At the beginning and end stand reflections on the life of Brother Lawrence, written by a man named Abbe Joseph de Beaufort, an influential churchman of that day. Between these two reflections stand de Beaufort's notes on four conversations he had with Brother Lawrence; sixteen letters that Brother Lawrence wrote; and a list of "Spiritual Maxims" that was found on Brother Lawrence's bedside stand after his death.

At times, Brother Lawrence's thoughts—recorded both by his own hand and by de Beaufort—may seem redundant. But

Brother Lawrence would not have minded that criticism, for his was a simple message: By continual recollection of God's immediate presence with us, we can actually live in that presence. This practice of the presence of God so transformed Brother Lawrence's life that he found that the usual monastic disciplines of spiritual retreats, spiritual direction, and even daily worship were no longer that helpful to him. It can be said that he transcended those more traditional modes of spirituality and prayer. Indeed, at one point, he claims that he actually transcended belief in God and achieved the pure experience of God.

No secret prayers lie at the center of Brother Lawrence's spirituality, and there is no special knowledge required. Instead, he offers this simple thesis: By disciplining ourselves to think of God constantly, we can place ourselves in God's presence. Or, to say it differently, we are already in God's presence, since God is with us and in us; our job is to be mindful of that presence.

This message has resonated with millions of readers over the centuries, and it will likely resonate with you, too. This little book is the legacy of a simple peasant monk from a long time ago, but it contains the very key to life with Christ that so many of us long for.

PRACTICING THE PRESENCE OF GOD

Brother Lawrence died on February 12, 1691. At his funeral two days later, this eulogy was delivered by Joseph de Beaufort, a prominent church leader in Paris at the time. De Beaufort had been inspired by Lawrence over the years, but Lawrence's spiritual brilliance was known by few others. This address at Lawrence's funeral served as the first introduction of Lawrence to the world, and his address was much acclaimed when de Beaufort later published it.

Eulogy of Brother Lawrence of the Resurrection

It is a consistent truth in the Scriptures that the arm of God is not shortened and that His mercy is not exhausted by our miseries. The strength of His grace is no less today than it was in the early days of the Church. It is His desire to perpetuate a life of holiness in men and women in every age. He always seeks out those who are willing to offer Him worship worthy of His greatness and majesty, and who, by the saintliness of their examples, can be models of virtue. He was not content just to place such people in the first centuries, but still raises up some from time to time whose lives demonstrate the worship of which He is worthy and are therefore a good example to others. These men and women, while retaining in themselves the first fruits of the Spirit, transmit that spirit to others and cause it to live in them as well.

The one whose life I would now call to your attention is Brother Lawrence of the Resurrection, a Discalced Carmelite brother whom God raised up in our time to render to Him all the honor that is due Him, and to quicken all Christians by the rare example of his faithfulness in the practice of all Christian virtues.

The "Discalced Carmelites" are the monks who go without shoes, the most severe and disciplined monks of the Carmelite order.

His name before entering the monastic life was Nicholas Herman. His father and mother were very upright persons who led exemplary lives, instilling in him the fear of God from his youth up. They took particular care with his moral training, teaching him only those holy principles that are in conformity with the Gospel.

He was born at Herimenil in Lorraine, where he had the misfortune of becoming involved in its military operations. While he was in the army, God was already showing him His goodness and mercy.

Herimenil is a small village in Lorraine, a county in northeastern France on the border with Germany.

Some German troops who were marching on a campaign took Nicholas prisoner and treated him as a spy.

In early modern France, peasants like Nicholas were often forced into military service. While only the aristocracy and the upper classes bore arms, the peasants carried supplies and often delivered messages across enemy lines. They were, of course, considered expendable.

He never lost his patience and tranquility even in such an unpleasant situation. They threatened to hang him, but he responded that he was not what they thought him to be, and in any case, since he was guilty of no crime, he was quite ready to die. And on hearing that, the officers released him.

The Swedes also made an incursion into Lorraine, attacking the little town of Rambervillers as they passed by it. There Nicholas was wounded, and he had to go back to his parents' home to recover.

This adventure caused him to leave the military profession and to undertake a more holy way of life under the banner of Jesus Christ. It was not the vain enthusiasm of an indiscreet devotion that gave him a distaste for the military. Rather, it was true piety that caused him to give himself wholly to God and gave him a desire to make amends for his past conduct. The God of all consolation, who had destined him to a more holy life, made him aware of how fleeting the world's vanities are and touched him with the love of heavenly things.

These initial impressions of grace, however, did not achieve their full effect at first. He often went over in his own mind the dangers of the military profession, the vanities and corruptions of this life, the instability of men, the betrayals of enemies, and the unfaithfulness of his friends. It was only after keen reflections, after a powerful inner struggle, after tears and sighs, that, conquered finally by the force of God's eternal truths, he made a firm resolve to follow the way of the Gospel. His uncle was a Discalced

Carmelite brother and it was he who made him understand that the air of the world is so contagious that if it does not strike dead all who breathe it, it inevitably alters or corrupts the morals of those who follow its ways.

While meditating on the promises of his baptism, the disorderliness of his youth, the mysteries of the Christian faith, and above all, the passion of Jesus Christ (about which he never thought without being inwardly moved), he was changed into another man. The humility of the cross seemed more beautiful to him than all the glory of the world.

Inflamed with a divine fervor, he searched for God in the simplicity and sincerity of his heart. His only desire was to be alone, so that he might weep for his faults. Since he was old enough not to have to reproach himself for any youthful haste, he thought more than once about withdrawing into solitude, and a favorable opportunity appeared.

There was a certain member of the nobility whom Herman knew whose noble birth and personal merit ought to have provided him with a satisfying life. Yet he was thoroughly dissatisfied with himself, always restless amid his riches. Persuaded that God alone could fulfill his desires, and preferring the poverty of the Gospel to all the treasures of the earth, this gentleman entered a hermitage. His desire was to taste there how sweet the Lord is to those who search for Him with all their heart. Herman, following his example, entered the hermitage as well. His soul was weary of the toilsome life it was leading and had begun to seek rest. Accompanied by his faithful friend, he retired into the wilderness, where the zeal for Christ within him dispelled his fears, and where he grasped ahold of God more than ever.

But although a hermit's life may be excellent for the advanced and mature, it is not usually best for beginners. Herman soon realized this, for the changing emotions of joy, sadness, peace, trouble of spirit, fervor and lack of devotion, confidence and despondency that ruled his soul, made him doubt the correctness of his path. He decided then to seek entrance into a monastic community in order to embrace a type of life whose rules, founded on the firm rock of Jesus Christ and not on the unstable sand of passing feelings, might strengthen him against the instability of his conduct.

In other words, Herman discovered that he was an extrovert. The solitary life in a hermitage didn't suit him, but, as we will see, the communal life in a monastery did.

Nevertheless, frightened by the prospect of an unending spiritual battle—and perhaps tempted by the devil—he found himself unable to make this decision immediately. Day by day he was more unresolved. Finally, listening once again to the tender call of God within, he came to Paris to ask permission to enter an order and there he became a lay brother among the Discalced Carmelites, taking the name of Brother Lawrence of the Resurrection.

From the beginning of his novitiate, he applied himself fervently to the practice of the religious life. He was most devoted to the Holy Virgin and had a son-like confidence in her protection. She was his refuge in all the difficulties of his life, in the troubles and the anxieties with which his soul was agitated, and it was his custom to call her his "Good Mother." He devoted himself particularly to the practice of prayer. However great his duties might be, they never made him lose track of the time set aside in the monastic day for prayer. The presence of God and the love He pours into the soul were his greatest virtues, and they made him in a short time the model for his fellow novices. By the victorious grace of Jesus Christ, he eagerly embraced penance and sought out the austerities from which nature flees with so much aversion.

The novitiate *is the beginning time of a monastic profession. A "tryout" of sorts, a novice may still opt out of the monastic life before taking on the full vows of the community.*

Penance *is the practice of confessing one's sins to a priest and then submitting to discipline (usually prayers) to show repentance. Following the time of penance, the priest offers forgiveness of sins on behalf of God.*

Although his superiors assigned Lawrence to the most abject duties, he never let any complaint escape his lips. On the contrary, the grace that refuses to be disheartened by harshness and severity always sustained him in the most unpleasant and annoying assignments.

Whatever repugnance he may have felt from his nature, he nevertheless accepted his assignments with pleasure, esteeming himself to be too happy either to suffer or to be humiliated by following the example of the Saviour.

The novice-master, sensing his merits and seeing the esteem he acquired by his courageous behavior, felt the need to test the genuineness of his vocation and the steadfastness of his spirit by increasing his difficulties, pressing him by different assignments. Rather than being put down by such experiences, or becoming disheartened by these trials, Lawrence endured them with all the faithfulness one could expect from him.

It seems that even during his novitiate, Brother Lawrence's superiors could hardly believe how devout and holy he was.

On one occasion, when a brother came to tell him there was talk of sending him away from the monastery, his response was, "I am in the hands of God. He will do with me what may please Him. I do not act out of respect to others. If I do not serve Him here, I will serve Him elsewhere."

When the time came for him to take his monastic vows, he did not hesitate. I could report here several beautiful actions that would convince the reader of the completeness of his self-sacrifice, but I will pass over them in order to emphasize the interior suffering with which his soul was afflicted. This suffering came about in part by divine Providence, which permitted it in order to purify him, and in part through his lack of experience and his wish to walk his own path in the spiritual life.

As he contemplated the sins of his past life, he was horrified. He became so small and contemptible in his own eyes that he judged himself unworthy of the slightest consolations of God. Yet he saw himself as extraordinarily favored by Him, and in the humility which his own wretchedness produced, he did not dare to accept the heavenly blessings God was offering him. He did not yet know that God is so merciful as to communicate Himself to a sinner such as he knew himself to be. It was then that the fear of illusion began to grip his heart strongly, and his spiritual state appeared so questionable that he no longer knew what would become of him. This doubt caused him such terrible torments that he could only compare them to the torments of hell.

In this trying state he would often go to a quiet place near his cell, where there hung an image of the Saviour attached to a column. There, he would pour out his soul before God, entreating Him not to let him perish, since he was putting all his trust in Him and had no other intention than to please Him.

A monk's bedroom is called a cell. Not unlike a prison cell, it's a small room with little more than a bed, a table, and a chair.

But no matter what prayer he made to God, his sufferings continued to increase, with such heavy fears and perplexities that his mind was suddenly unable to maintain control. Solitude, which he had regarded as a safe haven, had become a sea agitated with furious storms. His mind was tossed like a vessel beaten by the winds and storm, abandoned by its pilot, and he did not know which way to go nor where to flee. On the one hand, he felt a secret inner desire that was leading him to surrender himself to the Lord by a continual sacrifice of himself, and on the other, he was afraid of straying into error—which caused him innocently to resist God. All these thoughts filled him with horror, and everything seemed hideous to him. His soul was plunged into such bitterness and darkness that he received no consolation from heaven or earth.

As an extrovert, Brother Lawrence found that the part of the monastic life that caused him the most grief was not the hard work nor the long hours nor the rigorous prayers, but the solitude.

This situation, painful though it may be, nonetheless is what God often uses to test His true servants before bestowing on them the inestimable treasures of His wisdom. And this was what He allowed to happen to Brother Lawrence.

One cannot imagine his patience, his sweetness, his moderation, his firmness, and his tranquility in all these trials. Since he was so humble in his self-estimation and in his conduct, having only a low image of himself, he truly valued only suffering and humiliations, and asked only for the cup of the Lord, which he was given to drink in all its bitterness.

It might have pleased God to allow him to retain some of the anointing he had felt at the beginning of his conversion, but that was all removed from him. Ten years of fears and troubles gave him very little release. No pleasure in prayer, no softening in his sufferings: that is what rendered his life so heavy, and reduced him to such extreme neediness of soul that he had become loathsome in his own eyes and could not stand himself. Faith alone was his sole support.

Amid this throng of different thoughts, although reduced to the extreme, he did not lose courage. Rather, in the severest of his sufferings he always had recourse to prayer, to the exercise of the presence of God, and to the practice of all the virtues. He endured bodily austerities and long night watches, sometimes spending almost entire nights before the Holy Sacrament. Finally, one day before the altar, reflecting on the sufferings with which his soul was afflicted, and knowing that it was for the love of God and for fear of displeasing Him that he was suffering, he firmly resolved to endure them, not only for the rest of his life, but during all eternity, if that were God's will. "For," he said, "it no longer matters to me what I may do, or what I may suffer, provided that I remain lovingly united to His will, which is my only concern."

That was exactly the frame of mind God wanted him to have so He could flood him with His grace. From that moment on, the firmness of his heart increased more than ever; and God, who needs neither time nor human reasoning to make Himself understood, suddenly opened his eyes. Lawrence caught sight of a ray of divine light; illuminating his spirit, this light dissipated all his fear, and his sufferings ceased. The grace he received more than compensated him for all his past afflictions. Then he felt what the great St. Gregory said, that the world seems very small to a soul who contemplates the grandeur of God. His letters addressed to a Carmelite nun leave no doubt about it, and here is the essence of what they contain:

> Brother Lawrence had an epiphany, de Beaufort reports—today, we might call it a "spiritual breakthrough" or a "mountaintop experience"—where his loneliness and despair were replaced by love for God.

> Saint Gregory the Great lived from about 540 until 604. He began his career as a monk and was the pope from 590 until his death. He was a prolific writer of sermons, letters, and treatises. His writings were very popular in Brother Lawrence's day.

"The entire world no longer seems to me to be capable of keeping me company. All that I see with the eyes of my flesh passes before me as ghosts and dreams; what I see with the eyes of my soul is what I desire, and to see myself still too far away from it is the cause of my grief and my torment. Dazzled on the one hand by the clearness of this divine Sun of righteousness which dispels the shadows of the night, and on the other, blinded by my miseries, I am often beside myself. However, my most usual occupation is to remain in the presence of God with all the humility of an unprofitable, but nonetheless faithful servant."

This holy occupation formed his distinguished character, and his habit of keeping himself in such awareness of God became so natural that, as he explains in his letters, he spent the last forty years of his life in the moment-by-moment practice of the presence of God—that is, to use his term, in a silent and intimate conversation with Him. A religious superior asked him one day what means he had used to acquire the habit of the presence of God, a practice so easy and so continual to him. He replied with his ordinary simplicity: "From the beginning of my entrance into the religious life, I regarded God as the Goal and End of all the thoughts and affections of my soul. At the beginning of my novitiate, during the hours assigned to prayer, I spent my time convincing myself of the reality of this Divine Being by the light of faith rather than by the work of meditation and study. By this short and sure means I advanced in the knowledge of the One with whom I had resolved to remain always.

In this paragraph, de Beaufort lets us in on the key to Brother Lawrence's genius. Brother Lawrence's breakthrough transcended the traditional conception that prayer was something that a person engaged in at specific times of the day. Instead, he continually focused on God and therefore lived in God's presence.

"So filled as I was with the grandeur of this infinite Being, I went to enclose myself in the place that obedience had marked out for me—which was the kitchen. There, alone, after having made provision for everything connected with my duties, I spent all my remaining time in prayer, both before and after work. At the beginning of my duties, I said to God with a son-like trust, 'My God, since You are with me, and since it is Your will that I should apply my mind to these outward things, I pray that You will give me the grace to remain with You and keep company with You. But so that my work may be better, Lord, work with me; receive my work and possess all my affections.' Finally, during my work, I continued to speak to Him in a familiar way, offering Him my little services, and asking for His grace. At the end of my work, I examined how I had done it, and if I found any good in it, I thanked God. If I noticed errors, I asked His forgiveness for them, and without becoming discouraged, I resolved to change and began anew to remain with God as if I had never strayed. So, by picking myself up after my falls, and by doing many little acts of faith and love, I came to a state in which it would be as difficult for me *not* to think of God as it had been difficult to accustom myself to thinking of Him at the beginning."

As he experienced the great benefit that this practice brings to the soul, he advised all his friends to apply themselves to it with all the care and faithfulness possible. In order to make them undertake it with firm resolve and courage, he gave them such strong and effective reasons that he persuaded not only their minds, but penetrated even their hearts and made them love and undertake this holy practice with as much fervor as they had previously regarded it with indifference.

If he had the gift of persuading those who came to him by his words, he had it even more by his good example. One had only to look at him to be edified and to be placed in the presence of God.

He called the practice of the presence of God the shortest and easiest road to Christian perfection, the very form and life of virtue, and the great protection against sin.

He assured his friends that to make this practice easier and to form the habit of it in ourselves, we only need courage and willingness, and he proved this truth even better by his deeds than by his words. For it was seen, when he did his duty as a cook, that in the midst of an arduous task, even in the midst of the most attention-diverting duties, his mind and spirit were fixed on God. Although his duties were great and difficult, when he all alone did the duties that two brothers usually did, he was never seen to act with haste. Rather, with exactness and moderation, he gave each thing the time it required, always maintaining his modest and tranquil manner. He worked neither slowly nor hastily, remaining in constant evenness of mind and in unchanging peace.

De Beaufort is here establishing Brother Lawrence's reputation as the saint of the kitchen. That is, Lawrence went about his life, much of which was spent in the kitchen, concentrating on God's presence. He was assiduous and deliberate in his work, as de Beaufort records, because of his practice of the presence of God.

He fulfilled his kitchen duties with the greatest love possible for a period of about thirty years, until Providence ordained otherwise. A large ulcer appeared on his leg, obliging his superiors to assign him to a easier office. This change gave him more leisure to adore God in spirit and truth and more time to occupy himself more totally with His pure presence by the exercise of faith and love.

The intimate union with God that resulted from his faithful adoration and his practice of faith and love freed his imagination from its occupation with created things, difficult though this may be, humanly speaking. The powers of hell, though unremitting in their fight with humankind, no longer dared attack Brother Lawrence. His passions became so tranquil that he scarcely ever felt them. If sometimes they stirred up some little emotion to humiliate him, he was like a high mountain that sees storms formed only at its feet.

As you might guess, Brother Lawrence's "passions" were his *sexual desires, always an issue for a celibate monk. But de Beaufort tells us that this was hardly a problem for Lawrence.*

From that time on, he seemed to have a nature made wholly of virtue; he showed a gentle temperament, complete integrity, and a loving heart. His good physical appearance, his humane and affable air, and his simple, modest manner immediately gained for him the esteem and goodwill of all who saw him. The more often one saw him, the more one discovered in him a rare depth of uprightness and piety.

One of his notable characteristics was that he did not call attention to himself in any way. He always preserved the simplicity of the common life, yet without taking on a melancholy and austere appearance that would only serve to rebuff people. He was not one of those people who never bend, who regard holiness as incompatible with good manners. Rather, he affected nothing, was sociable with everyone, and always acted in a friendly, forthright manner with his brothers and friends, making no claim of distinction for himself.

Remember, Lawrence was an extrovert!

Far from presuming on God's graces and making his virtues seen in order to attract admiration to himself, he applied himself unwaveringly to leading a hidden and obscure life. For as the proud man studies to find all imaginable means to a high place for himself in the minds of others, one who is truly humble uses all his efforts to avoid applause and praise, and tries to discourage such praiseworthy feelings as others might have toward him. There were saints in ancient times who purposely did ridiculous things to draw scorn and mockery to themselves, or at least to inspire doubts about the worthy reputations they had gained. Brother Lawrence, too, made use of such devices. His humility made him feign behavior and adopt certain childish actions in order to hide his virtue and cover its gemlike brilliance. He was not looking for glory from such virtue, but reality, and since he wanted only

God to witness his actions, he therefore looked only to Him for his recompense.

Although he was so reserved on his own account, he did not hesitate to communicate his thoughts and feelings with his brothers for their edification—not the more enlightened ones, whose knowledge and reasoning powers often made them proud—but with the lesser and more simple ones. When he found some of that kind, he hid nothing from them. He opened to them with marvelous simplicity the most beautiful secrets of the interior life and the treasures of divine wisdom. The anointing that accompanied his words so strongly moved those who had the advantage of his conversations that they came away full of the love of God, desiring to openly put into action the great truths he had just taught them in private.

Since God led him more by love than by fear of His judgments, all that he said inspired this same love, urging his hearers to break the slightest attachment to the flesh and put to death the old man in order to establish the reign of the new.

De Beaufort is pointing to something that is just as compelling for us to consider today: Do we respond to God out of God's love or out of our own fear? God's love was clearly the impetus for Lawrence's life of prayer.

"If you wish to make great progress in the life of the spirit," he used to say to his brothers, "do not pay any attention at all to the beautiful words or the subtle discourses of the wordly-wise of the earth. Woe to those who look to the wisdom of men to satisfy their curiosity! It is the Creator who teaches the truth, who instructs the heart of the humble, and makes it understand more in a moment about the mystery of our faith and about God Himself than if it had meditated on them for many years."

For this reason he carefully avoided replying to anxious questions that lead nowhere, and serve only to trouble the mind and dry up the heart. However, when his superiors required him to say plainly what he thought about some difficult matter being proposed in a conference, he answered so concisely and straight to the point that his answer would silence all reply. That is what several knowledgeable men, priests as well as monks, noticed when they required him to answer them.

That is also the considered reflection of an illustrious French bishop on a conversation he had with Brother Lawrence. The bishop said that Lawrence had made himself worthy of inwardly hearing God speak to him and of having His mysteries disclosed to him, adding that the greatness and purity of his love for God made him live, even while on earth, like those who enjoy God's presence in heaven.

 The bishop to whom de Beaufort refers is Archbishop Francois de Salignac de la Mothe-Fenelon, a tutor to the French prince.

He lifted himself up to God by contemplating the Creation, persuaded that books teach few things in comparison with the great book of the world when we know how to study it as we should. His soul, touched by the diversity of the parts that make up the world, was lifted to God so powerfully that nothing was able to separate it from Him. He remarked how each of the world's different traits display the power, the wisdom, and the goodness of the Creator, and how these traits delighted his spirit, filling it with wonder, lifting up his heart with love and joy, and making him cry out like the Old Testament prophet, "O Lord, O God of gods! How incomprehensible You are in Your thoughts! How profound in Your designs! How powerful in all Your actions!"

He wrote such lofty and tender things about the grandeur of God, as well as about the inexpressible communication of His love to the soul, that those who saw a few detached sheets from his writings were so charmed and edified by them that they spoke of them with great admiration. He hesitated to lend these sheets and always on condition that they be returned to him at the earliest. This requirement, however, did not prevent a few fragments of them from being collected, and we can only regret that we do not have the others, for if we can judge all that he did by the little that remains to us of his letters and maxims, we have every reason to believe, as he himself declared to one of his friends, that his little writings were nothing more than outpourings of the Holy Spirit and products of His love.

He expressed himself sometimes on paper, but then, comparing what he had just written with what he was experiencing inside, he judged it so inferior and so far removed from the feelings that he had of the grandeur and goodness of God, that he often found himself obliged to tear up the papers immediately. He tore them up even more willingly because he had written them only to relieve himself of the fullness of his heart, to give release to his spirit, and to make room in his heart and chest, which were too narrow to contain the divine fire that was devouring him and making him suffer strangely—like a basin that is too small to hold its water and so lets it overflow, or like an underground place that cannot stop the violence of the fire in it, and so is forced to give it an outlet.

Faith was one of the principal virtues in which Brother Lawrence excelled. As the righteous live by faith, so faith was the life and nourishment of his spirit. It gave such growth to his soul that he made great and visible progress in the interior life. It was faith that had made him put the entire world under his feet, and made him scorn it and consider it unworthy of the slightest place in his heart. Faith led him to God, elevating Him above all created things, and making him search for happiness in possessing God alone. Faith was his great schoolmistress; and faith alone taught him more than reading all the books in the world could possibly do.

It was faith that gave him his high esteem for God and his great veneration of the sacred mysteries, especially for the most Holy Sacrament of Communion, where the Son of God dwells as a king. He was so lovingly attracted to the Blessed Sacrament that he spent many hours, day and night before it, offering homage and adoration to God. This same faith gave him a profound respect for the Word of God, for the Church and its holy ordinances, and for his superiors, whom he obeyed as representatives of Jesus Christ. Finally, he believed with such certainty the truths of faith that he often said, "All the beautiful speeches that I hear made about God, what I can read myself about Him, or even what I can feel—none of this could satisfy me. For since He is infinitely perfect, God is consequently inexpressible, and there are no terms with enough energy to give me a perfect idea of His greatness. It is faith that discloses Him to me and makes me know Him as He is. I learn more in this way, in a short time, than I would learn in several years of schooling."

> *The* Blessed Sacrament *is the Lord's Supper (a.k.a., communion* *or the Eucharist). The* ordinances *of the church are its rituals and rites, based on the teachings of the Bible and church tradition. Brother Lawrence's* superiors *were his abbot (the head of his monastery), the local bishop, and others, culminating with the pope in Rome.*

Crying out, he used to say, "O faith! O faith! O admirable virtue that illuminates the spirit of man and leads him to the personal knowledge of his Creator! O amiable virtue, how little known you are, and even less practiced, although your knowledge is so glorious and so spiritually beneficial!"

From this living faith were born his firm hope in the goodness of God, his son-like trust in God's providence, and his total and complete abandonment into God's hands, without causing him any worry about what would happen to him after death. He was not content, during the greatest part of his life, simply to rest his salvation passively on the power of God's grace and the merits of Jesus Christ; rather, forgetting himself and all his self-interests, he actively thrust himself headlong into the arms of Infinite Mercy. The more desperate things seemed, the more he hoped. He was like a large rock, beaten by the waves of the sea, which becomes stronger in the midst of a storm. This is what we have already observed in our mention of his interior sufferings shortly after his entrance into the monastic life.

If, as St Augustine says, the extent of our hope is the measure of how much grace we receive, what can we say about the hope that God imparted to Brother Lawrence, who, as the Scripture says, hoped against hope? This is why he used to say that the greatest glory we could give God is to totally mistrust our own strength and place our trust completely in His protection. This is the way to sincerely acknowledge our own weakness and recognize the omnipotence of the Creator.

 Saint Augustine of Hippo (354–430) is one of the most important theologians in the history of the church and is the author of The Confessions *and many other books.*

Since love is the queen and foundation of all virtues, imparting to all the rest their true worth and value, it is not surprising that Brother Lawrence's virtues were so nearly perfect, since the love of God reigned so perfectly in his heart. He had turned all his affections toward this Divine Object, as St. Bernard says. If faith made him regard God as the sovereign Truth, if hope made him envisage Him as his final End and perfect happiness, love made him regard the Lord as the most perfect of all beings, or more precisely, as Perfection itself.

Saint Bernard of Clairvaux (1090–1153) was a Cistercian monk. His conservative writings were popular in the seventeenth century.

Far from loving God for his own selfish ends, his charity was so unbiased that he would have loved God even if there were no suffering to avoid or recompense to anticipate, wanting only the good and glory of God and deriving all his joy from accomplishing His holy will (as we shall see in his final illness, when he had a spirit so free until his last breath, that he explained the feelings of his heart as if he were in perfect health).

The purity of his love was so great that he wished, had it been possible, that God had not seen the actions he was doing for Him, so that he could do them solely for His glory and without any return upon himself. He complained lovingly, however, and used to say to his friends that God did not let any of his actions pass without immediately rewarding them a hundredfold, often giving him such great feelings of His divinity that he was sometimes overwhelmed by them. He used to say, with his customary respect and familiarity, "It is too much, Lord! It is too much for me! Please give these sorts of favors and consolations to the sinners and people who do not know You at all, in order to attract them to Your service. As for me, who have the happiness of knowing You by faith, it seems to me that *that* ought to be sufficient for me. But because I ought to refuse nothing from so rich and liberal a hand as Yours, I accept, my God, the favors You do for me. Having received them, I beg You to let me return to You what You have given me, for You well know that it is not Your gifts that I look for and desire, but it is Yourself, and I can be content with nothing less!"

This purity of love and impartiality only served to set fire to his heart even more, increasing the flames of this inner divine fire, the sparks of which sometimes burst forth from him. For although he made every effort to hide the tremendous impulsiveness of this inner burning, at times he was powerless to do so. He was often seen, against his intention, with his face aglow. But when he was alone, he let the fullness of his fire burn, crying out, "Lord, give more expanse and more opening to the faculties of my soul, so that I may give more place to Your love; or else sustain me by Your all-powerful strength, for otherwise, I will be consumed by the flames of Your divine love!"

He often said, in talking with his brothers, regretting the time he had wasted in his youth, "O Goodness, so ancient and so new, I loved You too late! Do not do the same, my brothers! You are young. Learn from my honest confession of what little care I took to use my early years in God's service. Consecrate all your years to His love; I assure you, if I had known Him sooner, and if the things that I tell you now had been told me, I would not have waited so long to love Him. Believe and count as lost all the time that is not spent in loving God!"

Since the love of God and love for one's neighbor are one and the same, we can judge the love that Lawrence had for his neighbor by his love for God. He was persuaded from what our Lord said in the Gospels, that the smallest service rendered to the least of our brothers is counted as done to God Himself. He was particularly careful to serve his fellow monks in all his official duties, especially when he was busy in the kitchen. There, providing all that was necessary to their bodily nourishment, in conformity with their state of poverty, he took pleasure in making them as content as if they were angels. He inspired this same care in all who succeeded him in this assignment.

He assisted the poor in their needs as much as it was in his power to do. He consoled them in their afflictions, aided them with his counsel, and stirred them up to gain heaven at the same time they were working to earn a living. In short, he did to his neighbor all the good he could, and never did evil to anyone. He became all things to all men to gain all of them to God.

Here de Beaufort is comparing Brother Lawrence to the *apostle Paul, who wrote to the church in Corinth, "To the weak*

*I became weak, to win the weak. I have become all things to all
people so that by all possible means I might save some."*

According to St. Paul, love is patient; it triumphs over
all difficulties and suffers anything for the one it loves.
Can we doubt the patience of Brother Lawrence in his
infirmities, or his perfect love of God? In fact, if, according
to this same apostle, patience has a beautiful relationship
with love, so that love is the means of reaching perfection,
and patience is love's perfect outward expression, need we
say anything else to convince us of the state of perfection
to which God elevated Brother Lawrence? It is clear that
he exercised these two virtues in the midst of the very
painful sicknesses that God allowed to come upon him.
Besides a type of sciatic gout that left him limping and
tormented him for about twenty-five years and, having
degenerated into an ulcer on his leg, caused him very
acute pain, I will pause to dwell on three great illnesses
that God sent him in the final years of his life, in order to
prepare him for death and render him worthy of the
reward He had prepared for him.

*"Sciatic gout" and a leg ulcer sound like pretty horrible ailments,
and they were—especially in an era before modern medicine. De
Beaufort goes on to tell us how Brother Lawrence's great devotion
to God was even more evident during these illnesses.*

The first two illnesses reduced him to extremes, but he
endured them with admirable patience, and in the midst of
his sufferings kept the same evenness of spirit he had

shown in the most vigorous health. In the first illness, he showed some desire for death. Speaking to his physician, and feeling his fever diminish, he said to him, "Sir, your remedies are succeeding all too well for my liking. You are only retarding my happiness!"

In the second, he seemed not to have any preference at all. He remained indifferent to life and to death and was perfectly resigned to the will of God, as content to live as to die. He wanted only what God's divine providence should ordain.

But in the third illness, which separated his soul from his body to reunite it to his Beloved One in heaven, he showed the marks of extraordinary constancy, resignation, and joy. As he had been longing for this blessed moment for a long time, he conceived much satisfaction from its approach. The sight of death, which frightens and throws the boldest of men into the utmost consternation, did not intimidate him at all. He looked at it with a sure eye, and one can say that he faced it bravely. When he saw the humble bed that had been prepared for him, he heard one of the brothers say, "This is the end for you, Brother Lawrence; you must go away." "It is true," he replied. "There is my deathbed. But someone will follow me soon who scarcely expects it."

This very thing happened as he predicted, for though this brother who had spoken was in perfect health, he fell sick the next day, died the very day Brother Lawrence was buried, and the following Wednesday was buried in the same grave! It seems that the love that had united these two dear brothers during life did not want them to be separated in death, since no other place but that one could be found in the community burial ground.

Four or five months earlier he had said to several people that he would die before the end of February. He wrote two letters, two weeks apart, to a nun of the Order of the Holy Sacrament. At the end of the first letter, he said, "Adieu. I hope to see Him soon."

Adieu *means "farewell" and is more final. It is what one says when there is no expectation of reunion. Otherwise, one would say* au revoir, *which roughly means, "until we meet again."*

His second letter was dated February 6, two days before he fell sick. He finished his letter with these words: "Adieu. I hope by His mercy for the grace to see Him in a few days."

The same day he became bedridden, he said to a brother who was one of his close friends that he would not have a long illness, and that he would soon leave this world. He was so sure of the day of his death that the next day, which was Friday, he spoke more precisely, and told the same brother that he would die the following Monday. And that is exactly what happened.

But before telling of the circumstances of his death and the last views and feelings he expressed on his deathbed, let us go back to the constancy that he showed in his illness. His only remaining desire was to suffer something for the love of God. He repeated what he had said on several occasions, that his only sorrow was that he had not had any suffering, and he consoled himself with the knowledge that in purgatory at least he would suffer something to make amends for his sins.

Having found a favorable opportunity to suffer during his life, however, he did not let it escape. He purposely turned on his right side, knowing that this position was extremely painful to him, and wished to remain in that position to satisfy his ardent desire to suffer. A brother who was watching him wanted to give him a little relief, but he answered twice, "No, thank you, dear Brother. Please let me suffer a little for the love of God."

In this painful state, he said repeatedly, with much feeling, "My God, I adore You in my infirmities. O my Lord, I can finally suffer something for You. Wonderful! Thank You! Let me suffer and die with You." Then he would repeat these verses of the Psalm: *Cor meum crea in me, Deus; ne projicias me a facie tua; redde mihi laetitiam salutaris tui,* etc.

This is Psalm 51:10ff.: *"Create in me a clean heart, O God; turn not your face from me; restore to me the joy of your salvation. . . ."*

The suffering he experienced in this position, because of a painful place on his right side caused by pleurisy, was so great that he would undoubtedly have died had not the attending brother, who arrived at just the right moment, noticed it and promptly turned him over, restoring his ability to breathe. He was so eager to suffer that it became his entire comfort. He never seemed to have a moment of distress in the greatest violence of his illness. His joy appeared not only on his face, but in his manner of speaking as well. This caused some of the monks who visited him to ask him if, in fact, he was not suffering at all.

"Forgive me," he answered them. "I am suffering. This pleurisy in my side wounds me, but my spirit is content."

Pleurisy *is an infection which causes a painful inflammation around the lungs.*

"But, Brother," they replied to him, "if God wanted you to suffer these pains for as long as ten years, would you be satisfied to do that?"

"I would," he said, "not only for that number of years, but if God wanted me to endure my ills until the Day of Judgment, I would willingly consent; and I would still hope that He would give me the grace to remain always content."

So this is the patience that Brother Lawrence showed at the beginning and during the development of his final illness, which lasted only four days.

But as the hour of his departure from this world approached, he redoubled his fervor. His faith became even more alive, his hope more firm, and his love more ardent. One can judge the liveliness of his faith by his frequent exclamations: "O Faith! Faith!" he said repeatedly, expressing more in this way than if he had said many words. Penetrated with faith's greatness and enlightened by it, he adored God unceasingly, and said that adoration had become a part of his very nature. At one point he said to a brother that he no longer *believed* in the presence of God in his soul, but by the light of faith he could already actually *see* something of God's intimate presence.

The firmness of his hope was no less evident. His courage was so great in a passage where there is everything to fear, that he said to one of his friends who was questioning him about it that he feared neither death, nor hell, nor the judgments of God, nor all the efforts of the devil. He could actually see the devil circling his bed, but he mocked the devil!

Since his brothers took pleasure in hearing such edifying things, they continued to question him. One asked if he knew that it is a terrible thing to fall into the hands of the living God, because no one knows whether he is worthy of love or hatred.

"I accept that," he said. "But I would not want to know, because if I did know that I was destined for heaven, I would be afraid of being vain about it."

He pushed his abandonment upon God so far that, forgetting himself and considering only God and the accomplishment of His will, he said repeatedly, "Yes, if by any remote chance one could love God in hell, and He wished to place me there, I would not be concerned about it; for He would be with me, and His presence would make it a paradise. I have abandoned myself to Him. He will do with me according to His pleasure."

If he loved God during his life, he loved Him no less at the time of his death. He made repeated acts of love, and when a monk asked him if he loved God with all his heart, he replied, "Oh! If I knew that my heart did not love God, I would tear it out right this very moment!"

Although he was not left alone for a moment day or night, and although he was given all the help he might expect from his loving brothers, he was allowed to rest a little in order to profit from the last moments of life that are so precious, and to reflect on the great grace God had just given him in enabling him to receive all His sacraments. Therefore, he used those moments very profitably to ask God for the perseverance of His holy love until the very end.

When a monk asked him what he was doing and what was occupying his mind, he replied, "I am doing what I will do throughout all eternity. I am blessing God, I am praising God, and I am adoring and loving Him with all my heart. This sums up our entire call and duty, brothers: to adore God and to love Him, without worrying about the rest."

One monk commended himself to his prayers and pressed him to ask God to give him the true spirit of prayer. He told the brother that he had to give God his cooperation and do his own part to make himself worthy of it. These were the last views and feelings that he expressed.

The next day, Monday, February 12, 1691, at nine o'clock in the morning, without any agony, without losing his rational faculties, and without any convulsion, Brother Lawrence died in the arms of the Lord, and gave up his soul to God with the peace and tranquility of a person who falls asleep. His death was like a sweet sleep in which he passed from this miserable life to a blessed, happy state. For if one can conjecture about what follows death by the holy actions that precede it, how could we feel otherwise about Brother Lawrence? It is easy to conclude, without flattery, that his death was precious before God, that it was followed closely by an eternal reward, that his end is among the saints, and that he presently enjoys glory. With God, his faith has surely been rewarded by clear sight, his hope by eternal possession, and his earthly love by a heavenly, consummated love.

Joseph de Beaufort, the priest who spoke at Brother Lawrence's funeral, began to take an interest in the humble monk in the 1660s. De Beaufort met with Brother Lawrence four times in 1666 and 1667 and took notes after each conversation. He published them after Brother Lawrence's death.

Conversations
with Brother Lawrence

First Conversation
August 3, 1666

When I saw Brother Lawrence for the first time, he told me about his conversion at the age of eighteen before he entered the monastic life. God blessed him with an unusual and remarkable measure of His grace. One winter's day he saw a tree stripped of its leaves, and considered that sometime afterwards these leaves would appear again, followed by flowers and fruit. He then received a lofty awareness of the providence and power of God that never left him. This awareness caused him to become entirely detached from the world and gave him such love for God that he could not say whether it had increased during the more than forty years since he had received this gift.

> *This is a reference to the famous vision of Brother Lawrence: As a young man, he was feeling desperate and empty. One winter day, when he realized that the barren tree would once again grow new leaves, he also understood that he, too, would be*

43

*given new life by God. This marked the beginning of his journey
to become a monk.*

He continued the story of his life, telling me that he had
been the footman of Monsieur de Fieubet, the Treasurer of
Savings, and was a clumsy fellow who used to break everything.

He had asked to enter a religious order, believing that he
would be flayed for the clumsy actions and mistakes that
he would make there, and in this way would sacrifice his
life to God with all its pleasures; but God had fooled him,
since he had found only satisfaction. This made him often
say to God, "You have deceived me!"

He told me that we must establish ourselves in the
presence of God by continually conversing with Him. It is
a shameful thing to break off our conversation with Him
in order to engage in trifling or foolish talk.

*Here de Beaufort first tells us about Brother Lawrence's answer
to the question, How can we "pray without ceasing"?*

We must nourish our souls with a lofty idea of God, and
in this way we can take great joy in belonging to Him.

What we need is to make our faith come alive. It is a
thing worthy of pity for us to have so little faith, and
instead of taking faith for our rule and conduct, to amuse
ourselves with little devotions that change every day.
Making our faith come alive is the very spirit of the Church
and is sufficient to bring us to a high degree of perfection.

*Interesting point here, for Brother Lawrence's day and our own:
The spirit of the Church—that is, the reason for the Church's*

existence—is not to build buildings and bureaucracy or to keep clergy employed, but to make our faith come alive!

We must give ourselves entirely and in complete abandonment to God, both in temporal and in spiritual matters. We must find our contentment in the execution of His will, whether He leads us by sufferings or by consolations, so that everything should seem the same to a person who has truly abandoned himself. We must remain faithful in the dry periods by which God proves our love for Him. In this way we make fruitful acts of surrender and abandonment. A single act of this kind enables us to make much progress along the pathway.

As for the wretchedness and sins about which he heard daily, instead of being astonished by them, he was on the contrary surprised that there were not still more of them, considering the malice of which the sinner is capable. He prayed for the sinner and then did not trouble himself any more, knowing that God could change the sinner when it was His will to do so.

In order to succeed in abandoning ourselves to God as much as He desires, we must watch attentively over all the movements of the soul, in spiritual matters as well as in the most common ones. God gives light for those who truly desire to belong to Him. He told me that if I had this desire, I could ask to see him whenever I wanted without fear of being an annoyance to him, but without this desire, I should not come to see him at all.

Second Conversation
September 28, 1666

Brother Lawrence had always been guided by love, without any other self-interest, and he did not worry about whether he would be damned or saved. The goal of all his actions was to do them for the love of God. He found great satisfaction in doing this. He was even content to pick up one single straw from the ground for the love of God. He looked for God alone and nothing else, not even His gifts.

This conduct of his soul caused God to give him infinite grace, but while accepting the fruit of this grace—that is, the love that is born from it—he had to reject his pleasure in the fruit, recognizing that the end product comes from God but is not to be confused with God. By faith he knew that God is infinitely greater and more totally other than anything we feel about Him. So a marvelous struggle took place between God and his soul: God was giving and his soul was protesting that what it was receiving was not God. In this combat, his soul was by faith as strong and, yes, even stronger than God, since God could never give so much that his soul could not always protest that God was greater than His gifts.

In this paragraph, de Beaufort tells of a kind of spiritual wrestling match that Brother Lawrence has with God: He submits himself to God, expecting God to reveal Himself in return, but instead he received only spiritual gifts. Many of us would be content with this, but Brother Lawrence didn't want gifts, he wanted God Himself.

Ecstasy and rapture belong to a soul that amuses itself with the gift instead of rejecting it and going beyond the gift, to the Giver. Outside of feelings of surprise, a person should not allow himself to be carried away with his feelings, because God should remain the Master and center of our attention.

God recompenses so promptly and so magnificently all that is done for Him that Brother Lawrence sometimes wanted to hide from God what he was doing out of love for Him, so that, not receiving any reward at all, he might have the pleasure of doing something solely for God.

His spirit had been very troubled, and he had once believed with certainty that he was to be damned. No one in the world could have taken this conviction from him. But finally, he reasoned in this manner: "I came into the monastic life only for the love of God. I have tried to act only for Him. Whether I am damned or saved, I want to always continue to act purely for the love of God; I will at least have had this merit, that throughout my life I will have done everything in my power to love Him." This inner suffering had stayed with him for four very troubled years.

If Brother Lawrence worried for four years about whether he might be bound for hell, we might wonder who he thought was destined to be saved?!?

Since that time he worried neither about heaven nor hell. All his life was utter freedom and a continual rejoicing. He had put his sins between God and himself, as if to tell Him that he was not worthy of His grace, but that did not prevent God from flooding him with it. He felt as if God were taking him by the hand and leading him before the courts of heaven to show everyone the unworthy wretch whom it was His will to shower with grace.

At the beginning, we must somewhat apply ourselves to forming the inner habit of conversing continually with God and ascribing to Him all that we do. But after being careful to do this for a short time, we feel ourselves awakened by His love without any difficulty.

He expected that after the season of blessing that God was giving him, he would have his turn and his share of difficulties and sufferings. He did not let this worry him, because he knew very well that since he was unable to do anything by himself, God would not fail to give him the strength to endure whatever sufferings might come.

He always spoke to God whenever an occasion arose to do a virtuous act, saying to Him, "My God, I would not know how to do that if You did not enable me to do it." Immediately he was given strength, and beyond.

When he failed, he did nothing but admit his fault and say to God, "I will never do anything else if You leave me alone; it is up to You to prevent me from falling and to correct what is not good." Afterwards, he did not trouble himself at all about his fault.

We must behave very simply with God, and speak frankly to Him, asking Him for help in things as they happen. It had often been his experience that God does not fail to give His help.

> If Brother Lawrence's message seems to be getting repetitive here, remember this: He was neither a theologian nor a philosopher, but a simple peasant monk with a simple message. We can continually experience God's presence by constantly focusing our thoughts and affections on him.

He had been told recently to go to purchase wine in Burgundy, a task that was very painful and difficult for him, owing to his lack of skill in business and the fact that he was quite crippled in one leg and could not walk on the boat except by rolling himself on the winecasks. He did not trouble himself about his condition, however, any more than about the purchase of the wine. He said to God that it was His business, after which he found that not only was he able to complete his task, but it was done well. He had been sent to Auvergne the preceding year for the same thing; he could not say how he had done it, emphasizing that no credit should be given to him at all, and yet it was found to be very well done.

Burgundy is a wine-making region in east-central France. This was quite a journey from Paris in Brother Lawrence's day. And the old monk got himself around with his bad leg by rolling himself on a winecask!

Auvergne is a region in central France.

The same thing happened in the kitchen. Even though by nature he had a great aversion to doing kitchen work, he became accustomed to doing everything there out of love for God, and asked Him in every situation for grace to do his work. So he found that kitchen work became easy for him during the fifteen years he was assigned there.

Now he found delight in cobbling shoes, but he was ready to leave this task like the others because no matter where he was assigned, the thing that brought him joy was to do little things for the love of God.

For him the fixed time of prayer in the monastic day was no different from other times. He made his spiritual retreats when the prior told him to do so, but he did not desire them and did not ask for them, because even his busiest work did not turn him away from God.

Monks gather to pray at specific times during the day—these services are called the "daily offices." Some monasteries have three, but the stricter monasteries have as many as seven a day (starting at 4 AM!).

Since he knew that man must love God in all things, he labored to fulfill his duty before God. He felt no need of a spiritual director, but rather of a confessor, so that he could receive absolution for the faults he committed. He was well aware of his sins, and was not at all astonished by them; he admitted them to God, but did not plead his case as though he were in a courtroom and wanted to excuse them. Rather, having confessed them, he reentered into peace through his customary exercise of love and of inner adoration.

In his spiritual sufferings he had not consulted anyone; but with faith as his guide, and his only knowledge being that God was present with him, he was content to live and act for Him, come what may. He was willing to lose himself for the love of God, and in so doing, he found satisfaction.

The multitude of thoughts that crowd in on us spoil everything. Evil begins in our thoughts, so we must be careful to reject them as soon as we become aware that they are not essential to our present duties or to our salvation. Doing this allows us to begin our conversation with God once again.

In the beginning, he often spent the entire time of prayer set aside in the monastic day in rejecting thoughts and falling back into them. He had never been able to pray according to a rule like the others. Nonetheless, he would meditate for some time, although afterwards, he did not know how it had gone, and found it impossible to give an account of it.

He had asked to be a permanent novice, not believing that his superiors would find him fit to take his monastic vows, and hardly believing that the time of his novitiate had passed.

He was not bold enough to ask God for penances. He did not even *want* to do them, but he knew very well that he deserved to do a great number of them. Yet, he knew that when God sent penances his way, He would give him grace to do them.

All penances and other spiritual exercises serve only to bring us into union with God through love. After thinking a great deal about spiritual exercises, he found that it is even shorter to go straight to this union through a continual exercise of love, by doing all things for the love of God.

Although we might do every possible penance, if our penances are not done in love, they will not serve to erase a single sin. For our sins to be erased we must await the remission of the blood of Jesus Christ without becoming troubled or worried, laboring only to love Him with all our heart. God seems to choose those who have been the greatest sinners in order to show them His greatest grace, rather than choosing those who have remained in innocence, because this shows His goodness all the more.

He did not think either about death or his sins, about heaven or hell. His only thought was about doing little things for the love of God, since he was not capable of doing great things. Afterward, whatever happened to him would be according to God's will, so he was not at all worried about it.

To be skinned alive would be nothing compared to the inner pain he had felt, nor to the great joys he had so often experienced and was still experiencing. As a result, he worried about nothing and feared nothing, asking nothing of God but only that he might not offend Him.

Being skinned alive ("flayed") was a type of execution in the *Middle Ages. Tradition holds that the apostle Bartholomew was flayed, and Michelangelo depicts him holding his empty skin in the Sistine Chapel.*

He told me that he had scarcely any scruples, for "when I recognize that I have failed, I confess my failure and I say, 'This is my ordinary, my usual behavior; I do not know how to do anything else.' If I have not failed, I give thanks to God and confess that success comes from Him."

Third Conversation
November 22, 1666

He told me that the foundation of his spiritual life had been a lofty concept and reverence for God through faith. Having once begun this path of faith, his only desire was to reject faithfully all other thoughts when they began in order to do all his actions for the love of God. Sometimes he went a long time without thinking about God's love, but did not let this trouble him. He admitted his wretchedness to God and then came back with all the more confidence to Him. The more miserable he felt when he forgot God for a time, the more confident faith he felt when he returned to God.

Our trust in God honors Him greatly and causes Him to shower us with grace.

It is impossible for God to deceive, and it is equally impossible for Him to let a soul suffer for long who is completely abandoned to Him and resolved to endure all for Him.

He had reached the point of not having any thoughts other than of God, but when he felt tempted to flatter someone else, or had some other temptation, he felt thoughts that were not of God come to his mind. Yet the experience he had of God's ready help was such he would sometimes let them come. Then, at just the right moment, he would turn to God, and they would promptly fade away.

From this experience, when he had some outside business to do, he did not think about it at all in advance. When the time came for action, he found clearly in God what he must do at that moment. For some time he had acted in this way without worrying beforehand. Yet before this experience of God's ready help in his affairs, he used to think a great deal about them.

He did not remember the things he did, and was almost unaware even when he was occupied in doing them. On leaving the table he did not know what he had eaten. Rather, acting out of his one single aim of doing all for the love of God, he gave thanks to Him for guiding him in his work and in countless other actions. He did all this very simply and in a manner that held him fast to the loving presence of God.

When any outward duty distracted him even a little from thinking about God, there came into his soul a reminder from God that gave him an even stronger thought of God. This memory inflamed his soul and set him afire, sometimes so strongly that he cried out and sang and leaped about like a madman.

He was much more united to God in his ordinary occupations than when he left them to do the spiritual exercises of a retreat, from which he usually emerged in spiritual dryness.

An interesting point: Brother Lawrence so enjoyed his everyday life with God that spiritual retreats were often a letdown.

He expected to have some great suffering of body or mind as time passed, and his worst fear was that of losing the conscious awareness of God which he had possessed for so long. But the goodness of God assured him that He would not abandon him and that He would give him the strength to endure whatever evil He permitted to happen to him. Knowing this, he feared nothing and had no need to communicate concerning his soul with anyone. When he did try to communicate with others, he always came away more perplexed. Because he wanted to die and lose himself for the love of God, he had no apprehension or fear towards God. Complete abandonment to God is the safe path and is the way that enables us always to have light with which to guide ourselves.

In the beginning, we have to make an effort to renounce ourselves, but after that there is no longer anything but unutterable contentment. When we face difficulties, we have only to run back to Jesus Christ and ask Him for His grace. When He grants it, everything becomes easy.

It is a common thing to just be content to do penances and private spiritual exercises, forgetting about love, which is the end and purpose of it all. It is easy to recognize this by the works that such things produce and that is why so little concrete spiritual virtue can be found.

It is not necessary to have either a keen intellect or great knowledge to go to God, but simply a heart resolved to apply itself *to* Him and *for* Him, and to love only Him.

> In fact, Brother Lawrence might argue that it's more difficult for highly educated people to direct their minds and hearts to God. That is, we might assume that part of his spiritual acumen was due to his lack of formal education.

Fourth Conversation
November 25, 1667

Brother Lawrence spoke to me with great fervor and openness about his way of going to God, about which I have already written in some degree.

He told me that its essence is renouncing once and for all everything we recognize as not tending toward God, in order to accustom ourselves to a continual conversation with Him without a lot of head knowledge. All we must do is recognize God's intimate presence within us and speak to Him every moment, asking Him for His help. In this way we will know His will in doubtful things and we will do those things well that He is clearly asking of us, offering them to Him before doing them and giving Him thanks for having done them once we have finished.

In this continual conversation, one is also busy praising, worshipping and unceasingly loving God for His infinite goodness and perfection.

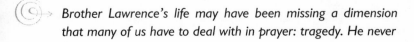

Brother Lawrence's life may have been missing a dimension that many of us have to deal with in prayer: tragedy. He never

seems to have struggled with God over the problem of evil (what theologians call theodicy); that is, if God is good, why is the world full of evil? And we never hear of him losing a loved one, etc. So, in this way, we might wonder what a life of practicing the presence of God is like when the praise and devotion is mixed with questions and tears.

We should confidently ask Him for His grace without regard to our thoughts, depending on the infinite merits of our Lord. Every time we ask, God does not fail to give us His grace. Brother Lawrence could feel this grace, and he failed only when he was distracted from the company of God, or when he had forgotten to ask Him for His help.

In doubtful matters, God never fails to give light when we have no other purpose than to please Him and do all for His love.

Our sanctification depends, not only on the changing of our behavior, but on doing for God what we ordinarily do for ourselves. It is a pity to see how many people attach themselves to certain deeds that they do very imperfectly because of their regard for human or selfish reasons. People who do that are confusing the means with the end.

Sanctification is a theological term for the steps in our salvation in which we become more holy in our behavior.

He found no more excellent means of going to God than the ordinary actions that were prescribed to him through obedience, purifying them as much as he was able of every human aspect, and doing them solely for the love of God.

It is a grave error to believe that fixed prayer times are different from any other time, for we are as strictly obliged to be united to God through our duties in their appropriate time as by prayer in its time.

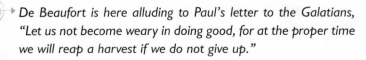

I feel a bit like Brother Lawrence when a worship leader says, "OK, let's start to worship God!" I think to myself, "I've been trying to worship God all day!"

His fixed times of prayer were no longer anything other than the practice of the presence of God, since his soul was at rest in God's presence, and was unaware of anything other than love. Outside these fixed times of prayer he found scarcely any difference, holding himself always near to God, praising and blessing Him with all his strength, spending his life in continual joy, yet hoping nonetheless that God would give him something to suffer when he was stronger.

We must trust God once and for all and abandon ourselves to Him alone. He will not deceive us.

We must not grow weary of doing little things for the love of God, who looks not on the great size of the work, but on the love in it. We must not be surprised at failing frequently in the beginning; in the end, we will have developed the habit that enables us to produce these acts of love without thinking about them, deriving a great deal of pleasure from them.

De Beaufort is here alluding to Paul's letter to the Galatians, "Let us not become weary in doing good, for at the proper time we will reap a harvest if we do not give up."

All we have to do is cultivate faith, hope, and love to attach ourselves solely to the will of God. We should be indifferent to everything else. We must stop at other things as if we were pausing on a bridge, passing over them very quickly in order to lose ourselves in our one single goal through faith and love.

All things are possible to one who believes; even more to one who hopes; still more to one who loves; and even more to one who perseveres in the practice of these three virtues.

Here's another allusion to Paul, this time to the famous "Love Chapter" in 1 Corinthians. It's interesting how reflection on these three virtues are at the core of Brother Lawrence's practice.

The goal we ought to set for ourselves is to be, starting in this present life, the most perfect worshippers of God that it is possible for a person to be, which is what we hope to do throughout all eternity.

When we undertake the spiritual life, we must consider in depth who we are, and then we will find ourselves worthy of all scorn, unworthy of the name Christian, subject to all sorts of miseries and to countless misfortunes that trouble us and make us unstable in health, in moods, and in our inner and outward dispositions. In short, we find that we are people whom God wishes to make humble through innumerable difficulties and labors, both inward and outward. Knowing this, should we be surprised if sufferings, temptations, oppositions, and contradictions on the part of our neighbor should happen to us? Should we not, on the contrary, submit ourselves to them and bear them as long as it pleases God, as things which are to our spiritual advantage?

A soul is all the more dependent on grace the more it aspires to go on to perfection.

Letters of Brother Lawrence

Sixteen of Brother Lawrence's letters survive, and they give additional insight into the practice of God's presence. They were written to other persons in religious vocations (priests, monks, and nuns).

First Letter
To the Reverend Mother N . . .

Reverend Mother is the title of a woman who is the superior of a convent, a women's religious order. In these letters, "N" stands in for "Name" to maintain the anonymity of Brother Lawrence's correspondents.

Dear Reverend Mother,

I have used the occasion of N . . . to share with you the views of one of our brothers about the wonderful effects and the continual help that he receives from practicing the presence of God. Let us both profit from these views.

Brother Lawrence is here referring to himself when he writes "one of our brothers." When he refers to himself in the third person, it is an expression of humility.

As you know, his chief concern for the more than forty years that he has been a brother has been always to be with God, and to do nothing, say nothing, and think nothing that might be able to displease Him, setting his sight on nothing else than His pure love, because He is worthy of infinitely more.

He is at present so used to this divine presence that he receives continual help from it in every sort of occasion. For about thirty years his soul has enjoyed such continual and at times such great inner joys that to moderate them and prevent them from showing outwardly, he is constrained to make childish gestures that seem more like madness than devotion.

If sometimes he is a little forgetful of this divine presence, God immediately makes Himself felt in his soul to call him back to Himself. This often happens to him when he is busily engaged in outward duties. He responds faithfully to these interior callings, either by lifting up his heart towards God, or by glancing sweetly and lovingly at Him, or by uttering a few words formed within him by love—such as, "My God, here am I; I am entirely Yours; Lord, do with me according to Your heart."

In this nice little prayer, we can get an insight into exactly how Brother Lawrence speaks to God.

Then he has the impression and can even *feel* that this God of love, content with these few words, goes back to sleep (as it were) and rests in the depth and center of his soul. The experience of these things makes him so certain that God is always in this depth of his soul that he has no doubt about it whatsoever, no matter what he might do, and no matter what might happen to him.

From this, Reverend Mother, you can judge what contentment and satisfaction he enjoys. Continually feeling within himself so great a treasure that he is no longer worried or uneasy about finding it, he is no longer suffering the pain of searching for it. He is entirely open to it and free to partake of it as he wishes.

He often complains about man's blindness and he cries without ceasing that we are worthy of compassion for being content with so little. "God," he says, "has infinite treasures to give us. Yet a little tangible devotion, which passes away in a moment, satisfies us. How blind we are, since in this way we tie God's hands, and we stop the abundance of His grace! But when He finds a soul penetrated with living faith, He pours out grace on it in abundance. God's grace is like a torrent. When it is stopped from taking its ordinary course, it looks for another outlet, and when it finds one, it spreads out with impetuosity and abundance."

Yes, we often stop this torrent because of the little esteem we show it. Let us no longer stop it, dear Mother. Let us examine our consciences, break through the dike, make way for grace, and make up for lost time. Perhaps there remains little time to us to live. Death follows us closely, so let us be watching closely for it. We will die only once.

Once again, I say, let us examine our consciences. The time is pressing, there is no more postponement. Each one faces death alone. I believe that you have taken just such measures, so that you will not be surprised by death. I praise you for that, for that is what our lives are all about. However, we must always continue to labor, since in the life of the spirit, not to advance is to fall back. But those who have the wind of the Holy Spirit sail even while they sleep. If the skiff of our soul is still battered by winds or by tempests, let us awaken the Lord who is resting there. He will soon calm the sea.

 Here, Brother Lawrence continues to talk to Reverend Mother about death (but he refers to it as "sleep"), and he makes an allusion to Jesus' calming the sea for the disciples.

I have taken the liberty, very dear Mother, to share these views with you in order to compare them to yours. They will serve to rekindle them and inflame them if, perchance, yours should become the slightest bit cool. May it please God that this should never happen, for it would be a great evil. So let us both remember our original fervor. Let us profit from the example and the views of this brother who is little known to the world, but is known to God and is extremely caressed by Him.

I will ask this for you. And, Reverend Mother, please ask this very earnestly for your brother in Christ, who is, in our Lord,

Your humble servant,

Brother Lawrence

Paris, June 1, 1682

Second Letter

To the Reverend Mother N . . .

Dear Reverend and very honored Mother,

Today I received two books and a letter from Sister N . . . , who is planning to take her final vows and has asked for the prayers of your holy community and for yours in particular for that happy occasion. She seems to me to have remarkably great confidence in the power of prayer, so do not disappoint her. Ask God that she may make her sacrifice in the sight of His love alone and with a firm resolve to be entirely His.

I will send you one of these books that deal with the presence of God. In my viewpoint, this is what the spiritual life is all about, and it seems to me that by practicing it properly, one becomes spiritual in a short time.

To become truly spiritual the heart must be empty of all other things, since God desires to be its only Master. And since He cannot be its Master without emptying it of all that is not Himself, He is prevented from doing all that He desires if it is not empty.

There is no manner of life in the world more sweet or more delicious than continual conversation with God.

They alone can understand it who practice it and savor it. I do not advise you, however, to practice it for this motive. The desire for spiritual consolation must not be our purpose in carrying on this practice. Instead, let us do it out of love for God and because it is His will.

If I were a preacher, I would not preach anything else than the practice of the presence of God; and if I were a spiritual director, I would advise it to everyone—so much do I believe it necessary and yes, even easy.

Oh! If we only knew how much we need the grace and help of God, we would never lose sight of Him, not even for a moment. Believe me; make a holy and firm resolve never voluntarily to withdraw yourself from God's grace from this time on. Live the rest of your days in God's holy presence, even if He judges it fitting to deprive you of all consolations of heaven and earth for the sake of His love. Put your hand to the plough. If you work as you should, be assured that you will soon see the fruit of your efforts. I will help you through my prayers, poor though they may be. I commend myself earnestly to your prayers and to those of your community, being to all, and to you more particularly,

Your humble servant,

Brother Lawrence

Third Letter
To the Reverend Mother N . . .

Reverend and very honored Mother,

I received from Mademoiselle de N . . . the rosaries you put into her hands. I am very surprised that you have not written me your reactions to the book I sent you since I know you must have received it. Practice its advice strongly now that you are old; it is never too late to begin.

I cannot understand how a person in a religious community can live happily without the practice of the presence of God. As for me, I keep myself at rest with Him at the depth and center of my soul as much as I can, and when I am with Him in this way, I am not afraid of anything. But if I turn away from God even slightly, it is like Hell to me.

This exercise does not kill the body. However, it is fitting to deprive the body occasionally and even often of little innocent and lawful consolations. You see, God does not allow a soul that He wishes to be entirely His to have any other consolation than Himself. That is quite understandable.

I am not saying that we must put ourselves under great restraint in order to do this. No! We must serve God in holy freedom, gently and tranquilly calling our minds back to God as often as we find them distracted from Him.

It is nonetheless essential to put our entire trust in God and rid ourselves of all other cares, including many private devotions. In themselves, private devotions may be very good, but they are often undertaken at the wrong time, since their purpose is to bring us to our goal. So, when by practicing the presence of God, we have reached our goal of being with Him, it is useless for us to return to the *means* of getting there. Rather, we should continue our love relationship with Him, remaining in His holy presence at times by acts of adoration, or praise, or request, and at other times by acts of self-offering, or thanksgiving, or by other ways our minds can discover.

Here again, Brother Lawrence distinguishes between means and ends. The practice of the presence of God is only the means; the goal is the actual presence of God.

Do not be discouraged by the reluctance your nature feels about doing this; you have to force yourself. At first we often think we are wasting our time, but we must continue in our resolve to persevere in this way as long as we live, in spite of all the difficulties.

I commend myself to the prayers of your holy community and to yours in particular. I am in our Lord,
Your humble servant,
Brother Lawrence

Fourth Letter
To the Reverend Mother N . . .

I think this letter is one of his best. Brother Lawrence says quite clearly to his correspondent (who is not a nun) that anyone is capable of practicing God's presence.

Madame,

I feel very sorry for you; if you can leave the care of your affairs to Monsieur and Madame N . . . and busy yourself only with praying to God, you will overthrow the power that presently governs your life and replace it with a better Power. He does not require a great deal of us; all He asks is a little remembrance of Him from time to time, a little worship. Sometimes we should ask for His grace, and sometimes we should offer Him our sufferings. At other times we ought to thank Him for the grace He has given us and which He is working in us.

In the midst of your work console yourself with Him as often as you can. During your meals and your conversations, lift your heart towards Him from time to time; the slightest little remembrance will always be very pleasant to

Him. To do this you do not need to shout out loud. He is closer to us than we think.

We do not have to be constantly in church to be with God. We can make our heart a prayer room into which we can retire from time to time to converse with Him gently, humbly, and lovingly. Everyone is capable of these familiar conversations with God — some more, some less. He knows what our capabilities are. Let us begin, for perhaps He is only awaiting a generous resolve on our part. Take courage, for we have little time left to live. You are almost sixty-four years old, and I am approaching eighty. Let us live and die with God! Our sufferings will always be sweeter and more pleasant when we are with Him, and without Him, our greatest pleasure will be but a cruel torture. May He be blessed by all. *Amen.*

So make it a habit little by little to worship Him in this way. Ask Him for His grace and offer Him your heart from time to time during the day in the midst of your work — at every moment if you are able. Do not constrain yourself by rules or private devotions. Offer him your heart in faith, with love and humility. You can assure Monsieur and Madame de N . . . and Mademoiselle N . . . that I am offering my poor prayers for them, and that I am their servant, and yours in particular, in our Lord.

Brother Lawrence

Fifth Letter
To the Reverend Father N . . .

Reverend Father,

I have not found my manner of life in books, and that does not trouble me at all. However, for greater assurance, I would be pleased to know your views about the state in which I find myself.

Several days ago, in a private conversation, a devout woman told me that the spiritual life is a life of grace that begins with servile fear, increases through the hope of eternal life, and is consummated by pure love. She also insisted that people have different degrees by which they finally arrive at this happy consummation.

I have not followed any of these methods. On the contrary, for reasons I do not understand, they made me afraid at first. That is why, when I entered the religious life, I resolved to give myself wholly to God in satisfaction for my sins, and out of love for Him to renounce everything that was not Himself.

In this letter, Brother Lawrence tells how he followed the traditional religious methods of prayer during his first decade as a monk, and how they didn't work for him. This led him to try practicing the presence of God.

During the first years I usually spent my fixed prayer times thinking about death, judgment, hell and heaven, and my sins. I continued in this way for several years. But during the rest of my day, even while working, I applied myself to practicing the presence of God, whom I always considered to be so close to me that He could be found in the depths of my heart. Doing this gave me such a high esteem for God that faith alone was capable of satisfying me. Soon, without being aware of it, I found myself doing the same thing during my fixed prayer times, and this gave me great sweetness and consolation. That is how I began.

I will tell you, however, that during the first ten years I suffered greatly. My fear of not belonging to God as I wished, my past sins, which were always present before my eyes, and the grace with which God was showering me— these were the material and the source of all my ills.

During this time I often fell, but I got back up immediately. It seemed to me that created things, intellectual reasoning, and God Himself were *against* me, and that faith alone was *for* me. I was sometimes troubled with thoughts that it was, in fact, out of presumption that I aspired to be suddenly where others arrive only with difficulty. At other times I had thoughts that all this was a scheme to damn me wantonly and that there was no salvation for me.

When I no longer thought that I would do anything other than finish my days in these troubles and anxieties (which did not diminish the trust I had in God, but rather served to increase my faith), I found myself suddenly changed, and my soul, which until then had always been troubled, felt a sense of deep inner peace, as if peace were in its very center and it had found its place of rest.

Since that time, I have been laboring to practice the presence of God simply in faith, humility, and love, and I have been applying myself carefully to do nothing, say nothing, and think nothing that could displease Him. I hope that when I have done all that I have been able to do, He will then do with me according to His perfect will.

I cannot express to you at present what is happening to me. I feel no suffering or any doubt about my state. I have no other will than that of God, which I endeavor to accomplish in all things, and to which I am so submitted that I would not pick up a straw from the ground against His order, nor out of any other motive than pure love for Him.

I have left off all devotions and prayers which are not required for me, and I occupy myself solely with keeping myself in God's holy presence. I do this simply by keeping my attention on God and by being generally and lovingly aware of Him. This could be called practicing the presence of God moment by moment or, to put it better, a silent, secret, and nearly unbroken conversation of the soul with God. Sometimes this conversation gives me great contentment and inner joy. But it also often gives me outward joy that is so great, that in order to restrain it and keep from revealing it, I am forced into childish actions that appear more like madness than devotion.

Finally, Reverend Father, I cannot at all doubt that my soul has been in the presence of God for more than thirty years. I am passing over many things so as not to weary you, but I believe that it is fitting to indicate to you in what way I consider myself to be in the presence of God, whom I picture as my King.

I regard myself as the most wretched of all men, torn with sores and full of stench, who has committed all sorts of crimes against his King.

As with much writing from the Middle Ages, it may be difficult to embrace the "King" language that he employs here, since we don't live in an era of monarchies. But, of course, kings were common in Brother Lawrence's day.

Touched with deep regret, I declare to Him all my evil deeds, ask His forgiveness for them, and abandon myself into His hands to do with me according to His will. This good and merciful King, very far from chastising me, embraces me lovingly, makes me eat at His table, serves me with His own hands, gives me the keys to His treasures, and treats me in everything as His favorite. He converses and takes endless pleasure in my company in countless ways, without speaking about my forgiveness or taking away my old habits. Although I implore Him to do with me according to His heart, the more I see my weakness and wretchedness, the more I am caressed by God. This is how I consider myself from time to time to be in His holy presence.

My most normal habit is to simply keep my attention on God, and to be generally and lovingly aware of Him. I often feel myself attached to God with sweetness and satisfaction greater than that experienced by a nursing child. Therefore, if I dared to use this term, I would willingly call this state being nursed by God, for the inexpressible sweetness that I taste and experience there.

If sometimes I turn away from this state through necessity or weakness, I am immediately recalled by an inner moving that is so charming and so precious that I am embarrassed to talk about it. I would ask you, Reverend Father, to reflect on my great unworthiness, about which you are fully instructed, rather than on the great grace with which God favors my soul, completely unworthy and ungrateful that I am.

My fixed hours of prayer are no longer anything other than a continuation of this same exercise. Sometimes I think of myself at these times as a stone before a sculptor, from which he wishes to make a statue. Presenting myself like a stone before the divine Sculptor, I beg Him to form His perfect image in my soul and make me entirely like Him.

At other times, as soon as I apply myself, I feel my entire spirit and soul rise without any trouble or effort and remain suspended and centered on God, finding its place of rest in Him.

I know that some will treat this state as idleness, deceit, and self-love. I admit that it is a holy idleness and a happy self-love, if the soul in this state were capable of that. In fact, when it is resting in this way, it is no longer capable of suffering the effects of things it used to do and which were its support, but which were harmful to it.

I cannot, however, allow it to be called deceit, since the soul that enjoys God in this state wants only God. If it is deceit in me, then it is up to Him to remedy it. Let Him do with me according to His will. I want only Him and I want to be entirely His.

I would be grateful if you would write and tell me what you think of what I have written, because I always defer greatly to your views, having particular esteem for you. I am in our Lord, Reverend Father,

Your humble servant,

Brother Lawrence

Sixth Letter
To the Reverend Mother N . . .

Reverend and very honored Mother,

My prayers, although they are of little value, will not fail you. I have promised to pray for you, and I will keep my word to you. How happy we would be if we could find the treasure about which the Gospel speaks! Everything else would seem as nothing to us. Since that treasure is infinite, the more we dig deeply into it, the more we find its riches. So let us keep unceasingly searching for it, and let us not become weary until we have found it.

Reverend Mother, I do not know what will become of me. It seems that peace of soul and rest of spirit come to me even while I sleep. If I were capable of suffering, it would be because I do not have any suffering, and if I were so permitted, I would willingly console myself with the fact that there is a purgatory, where I believe I will suffer to make amends for my sins.

Purgatory was believed to be the transitional state where believers
worked off their sins after death before ultimately achieving heaven.

I do not know what God holds for me; I am in such great peace that I am not afraid of anything. How could I be afraid when I am with Him? I cling to this assurance with everything in my power. May He be blessed in all things. *Amen.*

Your humble servant,

Brother Lawrence

Seventh Letter
To the Reverend Mother N . . .

Madame,

We have an infinitely good God who knows what we need. I have always believed that He would allow you to be reduced to extremities. He will come when He feels that it is right, and at a time that you least expect. Hope in Him more than ever; join me in thanking Him for the grace He is giving you, particularly for the strength and the patience He is giving you in your afflictions. This is an obvious sign of the care He has for you, so take Him as your consolation and thank Him for everything.

I also admire the strength and courage of Monsieur de N . . . . God has given him a good nature and a good will, but there is still a little of the world and a lot of youth in him. I hope the affliction that God has sent him will serve as a healthful dose of medicine, and that it will make him examine his conscience. This is a chance to encourage him to put all his trust in the One who is with him everywhere he goes. May he remember this as often as he can, especially in the greatest dangers.

All he has to do is lift up his heart. A little remembrance of God or an inward act of worship, even though he may be racing into battle with drawn sword, are prayers that, even though brief, are nonetheless very pleasing to God.

Here's another example of Brother Lawrence recommending to a "secular" person—in this case a military man—how he can practice God's presence.

Very far from making those who are engaged in military service lose their courage in the most dangerous situations, they strengthen them. So let him remember this as best he can. Let him little by little make a habit of doing this small but holy exercise. No one sees anything of it; there is nothing easier than to repeat these little interior acts of worship throughout the day. Please urge him to remember God the best he can in the manner I am indicating here. It is very suitable and very necessary for a soldier, exposed as he is every day to endangering his life and often his salvation. I hope that God will assist him and all the family, whom I greet. I am to all in general, and to you in particular,
Your humble servant,
Brother Lawrence

Eighth Letter
To the Reverend Mother N . . .

Reverend and very honored Mother,

You are not writing anything new to me. You are not the only one agitated in thoughts. Our mind is extremely fickle, but since the will is master of all our powers, it must call back the mind and carry it to God as its final goal.

When the mind has not been brought down at the outset, and has a few wicked habits of straying and wasting time, these habits are difficult to conquer. They usually draw us, in spite of ourselves, back to the things of earth. I believe that a remedy for this is to admit our faults and humble ourselves before God.

I advise you not to pray aloud much during your fixed times of prayer. Long speeches often become an occasion for straying.

I couldn't agree more! How many times have you heard some- one pray out loud and wondered whether it was a heartfelt prayer or a speech meant to impress the listeners?

Hold yourself before God as a poor mute, unable to talk, or as a paralytic at the door of a rich man. Busy yourself with keeping your mind in the presence of the Lord. If it strays and withdraws sometimes, do not worry about it. Worrying only serves to distract the mind rather than to call it back to God. The will must recall it gently. If you persevere in this way, God will have mercy on you.

One way to call your mind easily back to God during your fixed prayer times and to hold it more steady, is not to let it take much flight during the day. You must keep it strictly in the presence of God. As you become used to doing that over and over in your mind, it will be easy to *remain* at peace during your prayer times, or at least to recall your mind from its wanderings.

I have spoken amply to you in my other letters about the advantages that we can gain from the practice of the presence of God. Let us seriously busy ourselves with doing this and let us pray for one another. I commend myself also to the prayers of Sister N . . . and of Reverend Mother N . . . , and I am to all in our Lord,
Your very humble servant,
Brother Lawrence

Ninth Letter

To the Reverend Mother N . . .

Reverend and very honored Mother,

Here is the reply to the letter I received from dear Sister N . . . . Please take the trouble to give it to her. She seems to be full of goodwill, but she would like to go more quickly than grace will allow. One is not a saint all of a sudden. I commend her to your care—we should help one another through our words of counsel and even more through our good examples. I will be much obliged to you if you will let me hear news of her from time to time. Let me know whether she is very fervent and obedient.

We should often remind ourselves, dear Mother, that our only business in this life is to please God. What can all the rest be except folly and vanity? You and I have spent more than forty years in a religious order; have we spent them in loving and serving God who by His mercy called us to this life for that very purpose? I am full of shame and embarrassment when I reflect on the one hand on the bountiful grace God has given me, and continues unceasingly to give me, and on the other, on the poor use I have made of it, and my little progress in the path of perfection.

Since by His mercy He is still giving us a little time, let us begin in earnest. Let us make amends for lost time. Let us return with complete confidence to the Father of goodness, who is always ready lovingly to receive us. Let us renounce, dear Mother, let us generously renounce for the love of God everything that is not Him. He is worthy of infinitely more. Let us think about Him without ceasing and put our whole trust in Him. I have no doubt that we will soon experience the effect of trusting in Him, and that we will experience the abundance of His grace, with which we are capable of everything, and without which we are capable only of sin.

We cannot avoid the dangers and reefs that life holds without the very present help of God. Let us ask Him continually for it. How can we ask for it unless we are with Him? How can we think often about Him except through the holy practice that we must form within ourselves? You will probably tell me that I am always telling you the same thing. That is true! I know no more proper or easier method than this one. And as I practice no other method, I advise it to everyone.

One must be acquainted with a person before loving him. To be acquainted with God one must think often about Him; and when we do love Him, we will also think very often about Him, for our heart is where our treasure is!

Here, Brother Lawrence is quoting Jesus, who says, "Wherever *your heart is, there your treasure will be."*

So let us think constantly about Him. I remain, in our
Lord,
Your very humble servant,
Brother Lawrence
March 28, 1689

Tenth Letter
To Madame N . . .

Madame,

I have had much difficulty in resolving to write to Monsieur de N . . . . I am only doing it because you and Madame de N . . . wish it. So take care to put the address on it and make sure he receives it. I am quite satisfied with the trust that you have in God. I hope He will increase it in you more and more. We could not place too much trust in so good and so faithful a Friend, who will never fail us in this world or the next.

If Monsieur de N . . . knows how to profit from the loss he has suffered, and if he puts his whole trust in God, then God will soon give him another more powerful and better-intentioned friend. God disposes hearts as He wishes. Perhaps this gentleman had too much worldly attachment for the friend that he lost. We should love our friends, but without prejudicing the love of God, which must be first.

Please remember what I recommended to you, which is to think often about God in the daytime, at night, in all your occupations, in your exercises, and even during your times of amusement. He is always near you and with you.

Brother Lawrence again writes about a key to his thinking: that God is near. In contrast to some in his day (and ours) who consider God a distant and unapproachable deity, he considers God a close and intimate friend.

Do not leave Him by Himself. You would think it uncivil to leave a friend by himself who was visiting you. Why abandon God and leave Him by Himself? So do not forget Him! Think often about Him; worship Him without ceasing. Live and die with Him. This is the beautiful call in the life of a Christian. In a word, it is our joy. If we do not know that, we must learn it. I will help you by praying for you. I am in our Lord,
Your very humble servant,
Brother Lawrence
Paris, October 29, 1689

Eleventh Letter
To the Reverend Mother N . . .

Dear Reverend and very honored Mother,

I do not ask God for you to be delivered from your sufferings, but I am earnestly asking Him to give you strength and patience to endure them as long as it is His will for you to suffer. Console yourself with the One who keeps you fastened to the cross. He will free you from it when He judges it fitting.

They are blessed who suffer with Him. Get accustomed to suffering on your cross and ask Him for the strength to endure everything His will allows, for as long as He judges necessary for you.

The world does not understand these truths, and that does not surprise me. It is just that they suffer as people of the world and not as Christians. They regard sicknesses as sufferings of the flesh, and not as God's graces, and because of that they find nothing in them but what is contrary and arduous to nature. But those who consider their sufferings as coming from the hand of God, as effects of His mercy, and as means that He uses for their salvation, commonly enjoy in them such great sweetness and consolations that they can actually feel them.

> *He's making an interesting and controversial theological point here: our sufferings are actually gifts that come directly from God. Surely not all Christians agree with this point, but many do.*

I would like to be able to persuade you that God is often nearer to us in our times of sickness and infirmity than when we enjoy perfect health. Do not look for any other physician than Him. As I can understand it, He wants to heal you Himself. Put all your trust in Him. You will soon see the effects that we often delay by putting greater trust in medical remedies than in God.

Whatever healing remedies you may use, they will not be effective except to the degree that His will permits. When sufferings come from God, He alone can heal them. He often allows us sicknesses of the body in order to heal those of the soul. So be consoled with the Sovereign Physician of souls and bodies.

I foresee that you will tell me that I have it very easy, that I eat and drink at the table of the Lord. You are right. But do you think that it would be a small suffering for the greatest criminal in the world to eat at the table of the king and to be served by His hands, without, however, being assured of His forgiveness? I think that he would indeed feel such great suffering that only trust in the goodness of his sovereign could moderate it. So I can assure you that whatever sweetness I may feel in drinking and eating at the table of my King, I am tormented by my sins, which are always present before my eyes, and by the uncertainty of my forgiveness, even though in truth my suffering is pleasant to me.

Be content with the state in which God has placed you. However happy you may believe me to be, I envy you.

Pains and sufferings are paradise to me when I suffer with God, and the greatest pleasures would be hell to me if I enjoyed them without Him. My greatest consolation would be to suffer something for Him.

I will soon be at the point of going to see God; that is, of going to render account to Him. For if I were to see God for a single moment, the sufferings of purgatory would be sweet to me, even if they should last to the end of the world. What consoles me in this life is that by faith I do see God. I see Him in a way that could sometimes make me say that I no longer *believe,* but I *see* and e*xperience* what faith teaches us. On this assurance and this practice of faith, I will live and die with Him.

So keep yourself always with God. That is the sole and only comfort for you in your troubles. And in my prayers I will ask Him to remain with you. I greet the Reverend Mother Prioress and I commend myself to her devout prayers, to those of the holy community, and to your own. I am in our Lord,

Your very humble servant,

Brother Lawrence

November 17, 1690

Twelfth Letter
To the Reverend Mother N . . .

Since you have expressed such an eager desire to have me share with you the method I have used to arrive at that state of the presence of God in which our Lord by His mercy was willing to place me, I cannot conceal from you that it is with much reluctance that I allow myself to be won over by your persistence. I am writing only under the condition that you will not share my letter with anyone. If I knew that you were to let it be seen, all the desire I have for your perfection would not be able to persuade me to do it. Here is what I have to say to you about it.

I guess she didn't respect his request!

Having found in several books different methods for going to God and various practices of the spiritual life, I felt that they would only confuse my mind rather than make it easier for me to obtain what I was looking for, which was nothing else but a way to belong entirely to God. This made me resolve to give all for all.

So, after having given myself to God to make amends for my sins, I renounced for His love everything that was not Himself, and I began to live as if there were only He and I in the world. I sometimes considered myself before Him as a poor criminal at the feet of his Judge, and at other times I regarded Him in my heart as my Father, as my God. I worshipped Him there as often as I was able, keeping my mind in His holy presence, and recalling it whenever I found it had become distracted from Him. I had no trouble with this exercise, which I continued in spite of all the difficulties I found in practicing it, not becoming troubled or worried when I was involuntarily distracted. I maintained this practice no less during the day than during my times set aside for prayer. For at all times, at every hour and every moment, even in the busiest part of my work, I banished and dismissed from my mind everything that could take away the thought of God from me.

This, dear Reverend Mother, has been my common practice since I have been a brother. Although I have practiced it only with much faintheartedness and imperfection, I have nonetheless received very great advantages from it. I know very well that it is to the mercy and the goodness of the Lord that those blessings must be attributed, since we can do nothing without Him—myself even less than others. But when we are faithful to keep ourselves in His holy presence, to consider that He is always before us, in addition to the fact that this prevents us from offending Him or voluntarily doing anything that would displease Him, we are enabled to take the holy liberty of asking Him for the grace we need. Finally, by doing these acts repeatedly, they become more familiar to us, and the presence of God becomes as if it were a part of our nature.

Please join me in thanking Him for His great goodness toward me. I cannot praise Him enough for the great outpouring of grace He has given to such a wretched sinner as I. May He be blessed by all. *Amen.* I am in our Lord,
Your humble servant,
Brother Lawrence

Thirteenth Letter

To the Reverend Mother N . . .

Dear Reverend Mother,

If we were quite used to practicing the presence of God, all sickness of the body would seem trivial to us. Often God permits us to suffer a little in order to purify us and cause us to remain with Him. I cannot understand how a soul who is with God and who wants only Him is capable of suffering. My own experience proves this.

In this letter, Brother Lawrence deals with the issue of sickness and suffering, and considers how dwelling on God's presence can lessen one's afflictions. The Reverend Mother is suffering and, of course, Brother Lawrence has his own infirmities.

Take courage. Offer your sufferings unceasingly to Him. Ask for strength to endure them. Above all, make it a habit to converse often with Him and forget Him as little as you are able. Worship Him in your infirmities and present them to Him from time to time as an offering of sacrifice. In the worst of your pains, ask Him humbly and lovingly, as a child would ask his loving father, for conformity to His holy will and for the help of His grace. I will help you in this through my prayers, poor and weak though they may be.

God has many ways to draw us to Himself. He sometimes hides from us, but faith alone, which will not fail us in need, must be our only support. We must make our faith in God the sole foundation of our trust and confidence.

I do not know what God wills to do with me, but I grow ever more happy. Everyone suffers, and yet I, who ought to do rigorous penances, feel such continual and great joys that it is difficult to keep myself under control.

I would willingly ask God to allow me to share your sufferings if I did not know my weakness, which is so great that if He left me for a moment to myself, I would be the most miserable of all creatures. I do not know, however, how He could ever leave me alone, since faith makes Him so real to me that it is as though I am actually touching Him. He never draws away from us unless we first draw away from Him, so let us be afraid to draw away from Him. Let us always remain with Him. Let us live and die with Him. Pray to Him for me, and I will pray for you.

Your very humble servant,
Brother Lawrence
November 28, 1690

Fourteenth Letter
To the Same Reverend Mother

Dear Reverend Mother,

It gives me grief to see you suffer so long. What softens the compassion I have for your sufferings is that I am persuaded that they are proofs of the love that God has for you. Look at them in that way, and they will be easy for you to bear. My thought is that you should stop all human remedies and that you should abandon yourself entirely to divine Providence. Perhaps God is waiting only for this abandonment and perfect trust in Him to heal you. Since, in spite of all the care that you have taken, the remedies are not having the effect they should have, and on the contrary, the illness is increasing, it is no longer tempting God to abandon yourself into His hands and await what it is His will to send you.

I told you before in my last letter that sometimes He permits the body to suffer in order to heal the sickness of our souls. Take courage. Turn your need into a virtue. Ask God not to be delivered from sufferings of the body, but for the strength to suffer courageously for His love's sake, as much as He wants for as long as it is His will.

To be sure, these prayers are a little hard for our human nature, but they are very pleasing to God and sweet to those who love Him. Love softens the sufferings, and when we love God, we ought to suffer for Him with joy and courage. Do this, please. Console yourself with Him who is the sole and only remedy for all our ills. He is the Father of the afflicted and is always ready to help us. He loves us infinitely more than we think. So love Him, and do not seek any longer for any comfort other than in Him. I hope that you will receive it soon. Adieu. I will help you through my prayers, poor as they are, and will always be, in our Lord,

Your very humble servant,

Brother Lawrence

P. S. This morning, the Feast Day of St. Thomas, I remembered you and prayed for you as I took communion.

The Feast Day of St. Thomas was held on December 21 in Brother Lawrence's day. Today, the Anglican Church still celebrates St. Thomas in December, but the Roman Catholic Church has moved his feast day to July 3.

Fifteenth Letter
To the Same Very Dear Mother

Dearest Mother,

I give thanks to the Lord that you have received a little relief as you have desired. I have been at the point of death many times, but as I have never been so happy, I have not asked for relief. Instead, I have asked for the strength to suffer courageously, humbly, and lovingly. Take courage, my very dear Mother. Ah! How sweet it is to suffer with God! However great your sufferings may be, endure them with love. It is a paradise to suffer and remain with Him.

If we wish to enjoy the peace of paradise beginning in this life, we must become used to a familiar, humble, and loving conversation with God. We must keep our minds from straying on any occasion. For His sake we must make our hearts a spiritual temple where we worship Him without ceasing. We must unremittingly watch over ourselves so that we will do nothing, say nothing, or think nothing that would displease Him. When we are concentrated on God in this way, our sufferings will no longer contain anything but sweetness, anointing, and consolation.

I know that to begin to arrive at this state is extremely difficult, because we must act purely in faith. Just remember that we can do all things with the Lord's grace and that He does not refuse His grace to those who ask earnestly for it. Knock at His door and keep on knocking, and I assure you that He will open it to you in His time, if you do not become discouraged. I tell you further that He will give you all at once what He has put off for several years. Adieu. Pray to Him for me as I do for you. I hope to see Him soon.

Here he alludes to Jesus' saying, "Knock and the door will be opened; seek and you will find."

I am yours in our Lord,
Brother Lawrence
January 22, 1691

Sixteenth Letter
To the Same Dear Mother

My Dear Mother,

God knows very well what we need, and all He does is for our good. If only we knew how much He loves us, we would always be ready to receive equally from His hand the sweet and the bitter, and even the hardest and most painful things would be sweet and pleasant to us. The most difficult sufferings usually seem intolerable only because of the way we look at them. When we are persuaded that it is the hand of God which is acting in our lives and that it is a Father full of love who allows these states of humiliation, pain, and suffering, then all the bitterness is removed from them and they contain only sweetness.

Let us make it our business to know God. The more we know Him, the more we desire to know Him. And as love is measured by familiarity, the deeper and broader our familiarity with Him is, the greater our love will be. And if our love is great, we love Him equally in sufferings and in consolations.

Let us not search for God or to love Him because of graces He has given us, however extensive may be those already received or those yet to come. These graces, however great they may be, will never bring us as close to Him as faith brings us through a simple act. Let us seek Him often by faith. He is within us, so let us not search for Him elsewhere. Would it not be rude of us to leave Him by Himself? Are we not guilty of doing so, spending our time on myriads of worthless baubles that displease and perhaps offend Him? He endures them nonetheless, but it is greatly to be feared that one day they will cost us dearly.

Let us begin to be His in earnest. Let us banish from our hearts and minds all that is not Him. He wants to be the only One in our minds and in our hearts. Let us ask for the grace to make Him the sole object of our thoughts. If we do on our part what we can, we will soon see the change in ourselves that we hope for. I cannot thank Him enough for the little relief He has given you. I hope in His mercy for the grace to see Him in a few days. Let us pray for one another.

I am in our Lord,

Your humble servant,

Brother Lawrence

February 6, 1691

The Spiritual Maxims

Although Brother Lawrence often said that he wasn't a man of letters and that he found books of little help on his spiritual journey, it turned out that he had been writing some of his own thoughts down. Upon his death, some sheaves of paper were found in his cell, upon which he had written these "Spiritual Maxims."

All things are possible to one who believes, even more to one who hopes, and still more to one who loves; but all things are even more possible to one who practices these three virtues and perseveres in them. All who are baptized believers have made the first step on the road that leads to perfection, and will be perfect providing they persevere in the practice of the following guides to their conduct:

First. We must always keep our eyes on God and His glory in all we do, say, or undertake. May the goal toward which we strive be to become perfect worshippers of God in this life, just as we hope to be throughout all eternity. Resolve firmly to overcome, by the grace of God, all the difficulties found in the spiritual life.

Is it possible to perfectly worship God? Here Brother Lawrence calls us to the highest standard, just as the apostle Matthew did when he quoted Jesus as saying, "Be perfect, just as I am perfect." Maybe they're saying that it's the journey to perfection that matters, more than the destination.

Second. When we undertake the spiritual life, we must consider in depth who we are, and we will find ourselves worthy of all scorn, unworthy of the name of Christian, and subject to all sorts of afflictions and countless misfortunes. We will find that these woes not only trouble us but also make us uncertain in our health, in our moods, and in our inner and outward dispositions. In short, we will find ourselves among those whom God chooses to make humble through an abundance of sufferings and travails, both within and without.

Third. We must believe beyond any doubt that it is to our advantage to sacrifice ourselves to God and that He is pleased by our sacrifice. It is normal in His divine providence that we should be abandoned to all sorts of conditions, sufferings, afflictions, and temptations for the love of God, as much and for as long as it is His will. Without this submission of heart and spirit to the will of God, there can be no devotion or going on to perfection.

Fourth. A soul is all the more dependent on grace as it aspires to higher perfection, and the help and assistance of God are all the more necessary to us every moment, because without Him the soul can do nothing. The world, the flesh, and the devil all combine to make such a strong and continual war against the soul that without the very present help of God and our humble and necessary dependence upon Him, they would carry it away in spite of itself. To our nature this seems harsh, but grace takes pleasure in being dependent upon God and finds its rest in Him.

Practices Necessary to Acquire the Spiritual Life

First. The holiest, most universal, and most necessary practice in the spiritual life is the presence of God. To practice the presence of God is to take pleasure in and become accustomed to His divine company, speaking humbly and conversing lovingly in our hearts with Him at all times and at every moment, especially in times of temptation, pain, spiritual dryness, revulsion to spiritual things, and even unfaithfulness and sin.

This may be the most concise explanation of Brother *Lawrence's thoughts in the entire book.*

Second. We must apply ourselves continually to the end that all our actions may be little spontaneous conversations with God, coming from purity and simplicity of heart.

Third. We must weigh all our actions without the impetuosity or impulsiveness that mark a distraught spirit. As we carry out our duties, we must work gently, tranquilly, and lovingly with God, asking Him to accept our labor. Through our continual attention to God, we will crush the head of the devil and make his weapons fall from his hands.

Fourth. During our work and other activities, and even during our times of reading or writing, even though they may be spiritually oriented—and yes, even more during our outward devotions and prayers aloud—we ought to stop for a short moment, as frequently as we can, to adore God deep within our hearts and take pleasure in Him, even though we might have to do this momentarily and in secret. Since you are not unmindful of the fact that God is present before you as you carry out your duties, and you know that He is at the depth and center of your soul, why not stop from time to time, whatever you are doing—even if you are praying aloud—to adore Him inwardly, to praise Him, to beseech Him, to offer your heart to Him, and to thank Him?

What could please God more than for us to leave all created things over and over each day in this way in order to withdraw and worship Him in our hearts? Not to mention the fact that this is the way to destroy self-love, which cannot exist except among us creatures. Inwardly returning to God in this way rids us of self-love without our even being aware of it.

Finally, we can give no greater witness to God of our faithfulness than by continually renouncing and turning from the created things around us to take pleasure, even for a single moment, in our Creator.

Here we might wonder if Brother Lawrence is correct: couldn't some of the created things that bring us pleasure—say, a sunset—be gifts that guide us into God's presence?

This is not to suggest that you should withdraw inwardly forever. That is not possible. But prudence, the mother of virtues, will guide you. Nonetheless, I maintain that it is a common error among spiritual persons not to withdraw from outward things from time to time to worship God within themselves and to find comfort and pleasure in the peace of His divine presence for a few moments.

This digression has been lengthy, but I thought that the matter demanded all this explanation. Let us return to our discussion of spiritual practices.

Fifth. All this adoration must be done in faith, believing that in truth God is in our hearts, that we must worship, love, and serve Him in spirit and truth, and that He sees all that is happening or will happen in us and in all creatures. We must believe that He is altogether independent of everything and that He is the One on whom every created thing depends. He is infinitely perfect and is worthy by His infinite excellence and His sovereignty of all that we are and of all that is in heaven and on earth. We must believe that He can dispose according to His good pleasure in time and in eternity, and that we justly owe Him all our thoughts, our words, and our actions. Let us see that we do it!

Another important point, related to the theological concept of theosis: that is, God dwells within us, and the more attentive we can be to his presence in us, the more we will live the lives he wants us to live.

Sixth. We must study carefully which virtues we need most, those which are the most difficult to acquire, the sins into which we often fall, and the most frequent and inevitable occasions of our falls. We must run back to God with complete confidence when an occasion for spiritual warfare arises, remaining steadfast in the presence of His divine majesty, humbly worshipping Him and presenting our miseries and afflictions to Him, and asking Him lovingly for the help of His grace. By doing this, in God we will discover all virtues without having any ourselves.

How to Worship God in Spirit and Truth

Brother Lawrence is alluding to Jesus' conversation with a Samaritan woman, recorded in John 4, in which Jesus says, "Yet a time is coming and has now come when the true worshipers will worship the Father in the Spirit and in truth, for they are the kind of worshipers the Father seeks. God is spirit, and his worshipers must worship in the Spirit and in truth."

There are three answers to this question.

First. To worship God in spirit and truth means to worship God as we ought to worship Him. God is Spirit, so we must worship Him in spirit and truth, that is, with a humble and true spiritual adoration in the depth and center of our souls that God alone can see. We can repeat it so often that in the end it will become a part of our very natures and will be as if God were one with our souls, and our souls one with Him.

Second. To worship God in truth is to recognize Him for who He is, and to recognize ourselves for what we are. To worship God in truth is to recognize as a very present reality in our spirit that God is infinitely perfect, infinitely worthy of worship, and infinitely distanced from evil. He is infinitely greater than all the divine attributes ascribed to Him by man. What man, lacking in wisdom though he may be, could refuse to employ all his strength to respect and worship this great and infinitely worthy God?

Third. To worship God in truth is further to admit that we are entirely contrary to Him, but that He is willing to make us like Himself if we desire it. What man could be so imprudent as to turn himself away, even for a moment, from the reverence, love, service, and continual adoration that we most justly owe Him?

On the Union of the Soul with God

There are three kinds of spiritual union: the first is habitual, the second is virtual, and the third is actual, i.e., accomplished in the present.

First. Habitual union is when we are united to God solely by grace.

Second. Virtual union is when we have begun to unite ourselves to God and we remain united with Him as long as we continue our efforts.

Third. Actual union—present, sustained, ongoing union—is the most perfect of the three. As it is wholly spiritual, its action can be felt within the soul, because the soul is not asleep, as it is in the case of the other two unions. On the contrary, it finds itself powerfully excited. Its actions are more lively than those of a fire, more luminous than a sun unobscured by clouds.

With these words, Brother Lawrence connects himself to the long line of Christian mystics who promise a fiery union with God to the one who contemplates Him with the whole heart and soul. See the book The Cloud of Unknowing *for similar thoughts.*

We must be careful not to be deceived into thinking that this union is a simple expression of the heart, as in saying, "My God, I love You with all my heart," or other similar words. No, this union is something indefinable that is found in a gentle, peaceable, spiritual, reverent, humble, loving, and utterly simple soul. This "undefinable something" raises the soul and presses it to love God, to worship Him, and yes, even to caress Him with an inexpressible tenderness known only to those who experience it.

Fourth. All who aspire to union with God should know that everything that can delight the will and is pleasant and delicious to it serves to further this union.

We must all acknowledge that it is impossible for our human minds to understand God. In order to unite ourselves to Him, we must deprive our wills of every kind of spiritual and bodily pleasure, so that being thus freed, we can love God *in our wills* above all things. For if the will can in some way understand God, it can only be through love. There is a great deal of difference between the feelings of the will and the operation of the will, since the *feelings of* the will come to an end in the soul, whereas the *operation* of the will, which is the expression *of* true love, ends up at God.

On Practicing the Presence of God

First. Practicing the presence of God is the application of our spirit to God; it is the vivid recollection that God is present with us. It can be accomplished either through the imagination or by the understanding.

In this section, Brother Lawrence helpfully emphasizes how remembering God and God's presence is key to what he's driving at.

Second. I know a person who for forty years has practiced the conscious presence of God. To this practice he gives several other names: sometimes he calls it a simple action, a clear and distinct knowledge of God. Sometimes he refers to it as a blurred, indistinct sight, a general and loving gaze at God, or simply the remembrance of God. At other times he calls it attention to God, a silent conversation with God, confidence in God, or the life and peace of the soul. In short, this person has told me that all these types of the presence of God are only different ways of saying the same thing, and that the presence of God is now so natural that it has become a part of him. Here is how it happened:

Here, again, Brother Lawrence is speaking of himself in the third person.

Third. Through choosing in his will to frequently recall his spirit into the presence of God, the habit of doing this has been formed in him in such a way that as soon as his mind is free from its outward duties, and frequently even when he is the busiest with them, the uppermost part of his spirit or the highest part of his soul lifts itself without any diligence on his part, and remains as if it were suspended and firmly held on God, above and beyond all things, as if it were in its center and its place of rest. It is by faith that he almost always feels himself in this suspension, and that is sufficient for him. This is what he calls the state of being actually present with God, so that he now lives as if there were only God and himself in the world. He converses with God no matter where he goes, asking God for what he needs and unceasingly delighting himself in Him in countless ways.

Fourth. However, it is fitting to repeat that this conversation with God is done in the depth and at the center of the soul. It is there that the soul speaks to God, heart to heart, always delighting itself in God in a state of great and profound peace. All that happens outside seems to the soul like only a small fire that is extinguished as quickly as it is lit, with the result that outward things succeed to a very little degree or almost never in troubling its interior peace.

Fifth. To come back to our discussion of the presence of God, I maintain that this gentle and loving gaze upon God lights a divine fire in the soul without our being aware of it, and this fire burns so ardently with the love of God that we find ourselves obliged to do a number of outward things in order to moderate it.

Sixth. We would be quite surprised if we knew what the soul sometimes says to God, who seems to take such great pleasure in these conversations that He permits the soul complete freedom, provided that it wishes to remain always with Him and rely on Him. And, as though He were afraid that the soul might return to created things, God takes care to supply it so well with all that it can desire that over and over it finds deep within itself a source of nourishment that is very savory and delicious to its taste, although it never desired it or procured it in any way, and without its having contributed anything on its part other than its consent.

Seventh. We can conclude that the practice of the presence of God is the life and nourishment of the soul and that it can be obtained with the grace of the Lord. Here are the means of acquiring it:

The Means of Acquiring the Presence of God

First. The first means is leading a very pure life.

Second. The second is remaining very faithful to the practice of this presence and to the interior awareness of

God in ourselves. We ought always to do this gently, humbly, and lovingly, without allowing ourselves to be troubled or worried.

Third. We must take care to glance inwardly toward God, even for a moment, before proceeding with our outward actions. Then, as we go about our duties, we must continue to gaze upon God from time to time. And finally, we must finish all our actions looking to God. As time and much labor are necessary to acquire this practice, we must not be discouraged when we fail in it, because the habit is formed only with difficulty; but when it is formed, everything we do we will do with pleasure.

Is it not right that the heart, which is the first member to be quickened to life in us, and which dominates over the other members of our body, should be the first and the last part of us to love and worship God, as we begin or end our spiritual and bodily actions? It is in the heart that we should carefully produce this brief interior glance, which we must do, as I have said before, without struggling or studying to make it easier.

By the heart, Brother Lawrence does not so much mean the organ that pumps blood, but more importantly, he refers here to the seat of the emotions and the spirit.

Fourth. It would not be out of place for those who are beginning this practice to inwardly form a few words. We could say, "My God, I am entirely yours; God of love, I love You with all my heart; Lord, do with me according to

Your heart," or some other words that love produces spontaneously. But those who are beginning should be wary lest their minds should stray and return to the creature when they should be keeping them on God alone. When their minds are pressed in this way and constrained by their wills, they will be forced to remain with God.

Fifth. Practicing the presence of God is a little difficult in the beginning, but when it is done faithfully, it secretly works marvelous effects in the soul, brings a flood of graces from the Lord, and leads it without its knowledge to gaze simply and lovingly at God and find His presence everywhere. This gaze is the easiest, the most holy, the most solid, and the most effective type of prayer.

Sixth. Please notice that to arrive at this state, we have to mortify our senses, since it is impossible for a soul that still has some creature satisfaction to fully enjoy this divine presence. To be with God, one must absolutely leave all created things behind.

The Usefulness of Practicing the Presence of God

First. The first useful thing that the soul receives from practicing the presence of God is a faith that is more alive and more active in every aspect of our lives, particularly in our areas of need. Living this way easily obtains grace for us in our temptations and in the inevitable contact we have with created things. The soul that is accustomed to exercising its faith through this practice sees and feels

God's presence by simply remembering God. It invokes Him easily and effectively, and obtains what it needs. By doing this it somewhat approaches the state of those who are already enjoying God's presence in heaven. The more it advances, the more its faith becomes alive, and finally, its faith becomes so penetrating that it could almost say, "I no longer *believe; I see* and I *experience.*"

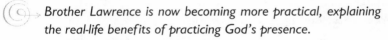

Brother Lawrence is now becoming more practical, explaining the real-life benefits of practicing God's presence.

It's interesting to contemplate this challenge: that by practicing God's presence, we can actually transcend belief.

Second. The practice of the presence of God strengthens our hope. Our hope increases as our spiritual knowledge increases, as our faith lays hold of the very secrets of God. By finding in God a beauty surpassing not only physical bodies on earth, but the beauty of the most perfect souls and of angels, our hope is strengthened. It is reassured by the very greatness of the blessing to which it aspires and that it sometimes actually foretastes.

Third. Practicing the presence of God inspires in the will a disdain of created things and sets it ablaze with the fire of sacred love. Being always with God who is a consuming fire, this fire of sacred love reduces to ashes all that can be opposed to it. The soul, so kindled, can no longer live except in the presence of its God. This divine presence produces in the heart a holy ardor, a sacred zeal, and a passionate desire to see God loved, known, served, and worshipped by all creation.

Fourth. By practicing the presence of God and by gazing inwardly at Him, the soul so familiarizes itself with God that it spends almost all its life in continual acts of love, adoration, contrition, confidence, thanksgiving, offering, beseeching, and all other excellent virtues. All these acts may even sometimes merge to become nothing less than one single continuing act that no longer comes and goes, because the soul is always in God's divine presence.

I know that there are few people who arrive at this stage; it is a special grace with which God favors only a few chosen souls, since in the end, this steady, simple gaze is a gift from His generous hand. But I will say, for the consolation of those who wish to embrace this holy practice, that He ordinarily gives this gift to souls who prepare themselves for it. If He does not give it, we can at least, with the help of His ordinary grace, acquire by the practice of the presence of God a state of prayer that comes very close to this simple, continual vision of God.

Brother Lawrence's Way of Life

M. L'Abbé Joseph de Beaufort
Grand Vicar of the Cardinal of Noailles

A couple of years after Brother Lawrence's death, as his writings were becoming more popular, de Beaufort wrote this short memoir reflecting on Brother Lawrence's legacy and included it with the other published material.

I am writing what I myself heard and saw of the way of life of Brother Lawrence of blessed memory, a Discalced Carmelite who died in the monastery at Paris about two years ago.

Although the public has already been given a eulogy and some letters, I feel that one cannot too often repeat those things that we have preserved from this saintly man.

I believe that it would be useful to show him as an excellent model of devotion to God in a time when almost everyone places virtue where it is not and takes false routes to arrive at it.

It will be Brother Lawrence himself who will speak. I can give you his very words from the conversations I had with him, because I used to write them down as soon as I left him. No one portrays saints better than they themselves. The *Confessions* and *Letters* of St. Augustine make a much more natural portrait of him than anything someone else could say about him. So nothing could make you better understand the servant of God whose virtues I would propose for you to follow than what he himself said in the simplicity of his heart.

The moral excellence of Brother Lawrence did not make him at all unsociable. He had a very warm manner that inspired confidence, making one feel from the outset that one could disclose everything to him and that one had found a friend. For his own part, when he knew those with whom he was speaking, he spoke with freedom and showed great kindness. What he said was simple, but always correct and full of common sense. Beneath a coarse exterior, one found a singular wisdom, a freedom far beyond that of a poor lay brother, and a depth which surpassed all that could be expected of him.

I find this excellent to hear. For all of Brother Lawrence's talk of ignoring everything around him and focusing only on God, it seems that he really was attentive to his friends as well.

He showed a mind capable of conducting great affairs, which one could consult about everything. Such was the outward appearance of Brother Lawrence.

He himself explained his frame of mind and his inner conduct in the conversations I will relate to you. His conversion began, as you will find stated in these interviews, with a noble and lofty conception of the power and wisdom of God, which he cultivated carefully by faithfully dismissing all other thoughts.

The conversations and interviews that de Beaufort mentions here are found in the "Conversations" section of this book, beginning on page 43.

Since that first revelation of God became in time the foundation of his holiness, it is proper to pause here to examine it.

Faith was the only light he used to know God. Not just at the beginning, but never afterward did he try to use anything but faith to instruct and guide himself in all the ways of God. He told me several times that all he had heard others say and all that he found in books — indeed, all that he himself had written, seemed pointless in comparison with what faith revealed to him about the greatness of God and of Jesus Christ.

"He alone," he used to say, "is capable of making Himself known to us as He is. We search in reasoning and in the sciences, as in a poor copy, what we neglect to see in an excellent Original. God paints His own portrait in the depths of our souls, and yet we do not want to see Him there. We leave Him alone in order to engage in foolish arguments, and we disdain to converse with our King, who is always present in us.

"It is not enough," he continues, "to love God and to know Him only by what books tell us about Him, by what we feel about Him in our souls, by fleeting feelings of devotion, or by some sort of personal spiritual illumination. We must make our faith alive and by faith rise above our feelings, to adore God and Jesus Christ in all Their divine perfections, such as They are in Themselves. This way of faith is the spirit of the Church, and it is all we need to arrive at a high degree of perfection."

Not only did he habitually contemplate God, who by faith was present in his soul, but in all that he saw and in all that happened, he lifted his thoughts immediately, passing from the creature to the Creator. A tree which he saw dry in winter made him suddenly lift his heart to God, and inspired in him such a sublime acquaintance with God that it was as strong and alive in his soul after forty years as the moment he received it. So he made use of this faith knowledge at all times, using visible things only to see what is invisible.

For the same reason, in the little reading he did, he preferred the holy Gospels to all other books, because he found in Jesus Christ's own words a way to nourish his faith more simply and purely.

This, too, is good to hear. While we don't often hear Brother Lawrence quoting the Bible, he clearly alludes to it as a result of his regular reading of Scripture.

It was by steadfastness in cultivating this high sense of the presence of God by faith that Brother Lawrence began. He talked with Him in continual acts of adoration and love, invoking the help of our Lord in what he had to do. He thanked Him after doing it, and asked His forgiveness for his negligences by admitting them, as he used to say, without "pleading guilty to a lesser charge." And since these acts of devotion were closely linked with his duties and since the duties furnished him with the material for his acts of devotion, he did them all the more easily, and, far from turning him aside from his work, they helped him do it well.

He confessed nonetheless that he had difficulty with this way of life at first and that he used to go for considerable lengths of time without remembering the presence of God; but after humbly admitting his fault, he began it once again without trouble.

Sometimes a crowd of unruly thoughts would violently shove out his thoughts of God. He would then simply push them gently aside in order to return to his normal conversation with God. Finally, his perseverance was rewarded with a continual remembrance of God. His different and varied acts were changed into a simple vision of God, into an illumined love, into an enjoyment without interruption.

Christian mystics agree that when a distracting thought comes into your mind during prayer, don't respond with anger or frustration, but gently repel the thought and move back into prayer.

"The time of business," he used to say, "is no different from the time of prayer. I possess God as tranquilly in the noise and clatter of my kitchen, where sometimes several people ask me different things at the same time, as if I were on my knees before the Blessed Sacrament. My faith sometimes becomes so dazzling that I think I have lost it. It seems to me that the curtain of darkness is lifted and that the endless, cloudless day of the other life is beginning to appear."

That is where the faithfulness of this dear brother in rejecting any other thought in order to attend to a continual conversation with God had brought him. He had made it become so familiar that he used to say that it seemed impossible to turn aside from it and be concerned with anything else.

You will find in his conversations an important remark on this subject, when he says that the presence of God should be maintained in the heart by love rather than by the understanding or by speech.

"In the way of God, thoughts count very little," he said. "Love does it all."

"And it is not necessary to have great things to do," he continues. (I am portraying for you a lay brother in the kitchen. Permit me to use his own expressions.) "I turn over my little omelet in the frying pan for the love of God. When it is finished, if I have nothing to do, I prostrate myself on the ground and adore my God from whom the grace came to make it. After that, I get back up, more content than a king. When I cannot do anything else, it is enough for me to have picked up a straw from the ground for the love of God."

"People search for methods," he continued, "to learn to love God. They wish to arrive at it by I do not know how many practices. They make painful attempts to remain in the presence of God by a multitude of methods. Is it not much shorter and more direct to do everything for the love of God, to use every one of our duties to show that love to Him, and to maintain His presence in us by the communion of our hearts with Him? We do not need to be clear; all we need is to have a good go at it." (I am religiously preserving his usual expressions.)

We must not persuade ourselves, however, that to love God it is enough to offer Him our works, to invoke His help, and to produce acts of love. Brother Lawrence only arrived at this state of perfect love because from the very beginning he had been careful to do nothing that could displease God. He had renounced everything but Him, and he had entirely forsaken himself.

"Since my entry into the monastic life," (these are his words) "I no longer think about virtue nor about my salvation. After giving myself entirely to God to make amends for my sins, and renouncing all that is not God out of love for Him, I came to believe that I no longer had anything to do the rest of my life except to live as if there were no one in the world but God and me."

So this is how Brother Lawrence began. He did the most perfect thing: he left everything for God, and did everything for love of Him. He had entirely forgotten himself. He no longer thought about heaven or hell, about his past sins or about those he was presently committing, after he had asked God's forgiveness for them. He never looked back on his confessions. He entered into perfect peace when he had confessed his faults before God, and he knew how to do nothing else. Afterward, he abandoned himself to God, as he used to say, "for life and death, for time and eternity."

"We are made for God alone," he used to say. "He could not find it wrong for us to abandon ourselves in order to concentrate on Him. In Him we can see what we lack better than we can perceive it by pondering about ourselves. These ponderings could not be anything but a vestige of self-love that still clings to us, attempting to look like perfection but actually hindering us from lifting ourselves to God."

Brother Lawrence used to say that in the great suffering he experienced for four years—so great that everyone in the world could not have shaken the conviction that he would be damned—he had not changed his first determination in any way. Without speculating about what might happen to him, and without worrying about his suffering, he had consoled himself by saying, "Let happen what may. I will at least do all my actions for the love of God for the rest of my life." So by forgetting himself, he had tried to lose himself for God, and had derived much benefit from this resolve.

The love of the will of God had replaced the attachment one ordinarily has to one's own will. He no longer saw anything in all that happened to him but the plan of God, which kept him in continual peace. When someone would tell him about some great sin that another had fallen into, instead of being astonished by it, on the contrary, he was surprised that it was not much worse, knowing the malice of which the sinner is capable. But immediately, he would direct his thoughts to God, knowing that He could set it right, and yet knowing that He permits general order of His governance of the world. After praying for those involved, he did not worry about it anymore, and remained in peace.

I told him one day, without any advance warning, that a matter of great consequence, which was dear to his heart and on which he had been working for a long time, could not be executed, and that a different resolution had just been taken. His answer to me was simply, "I must believe that those who have decided that matter have good reason, so there is nothing to do but to carry out their decision and say nothing further about it." That is exactly what he did, and so entirely that, although he often had the opportunity to speak of it afterwards, he never opened his mouth about it again.

A very worthy man went to see Brother Lawrence in the midst of a serious illness and asked him what he would choose if God offered him the choice of leaving him some time in life so as to increase his merits, or receiving him immediately into heaven. The good brother, without deliberating, answered that he would leave this choice to God, and that as far as he was concerned, he had nothing to do with it other than to wait in peace for God to indicate His will to him.

This disposition left him in such great indifference to everything, and in such complete freedom, that it approached that of the Blessed. He was not of any party or faction and took no sides. There could be found no leaning or opinions about temporal matters in him.

The Blessed is a term for those who have already died and experienced the joy of God's presence in heaven.

The natural attachment that one bears, even in the holiest of places, for one's own native country did not concern him. He was equally loved by those who held opposite inclinations. His desire was for the good of all, without respect to the people by whom or for whom it was done. A citizen of heaven, nothing tied him down to the earth. His views were not limited to time. By contemplating for a long time on the Eternal One, he had become eternal like Him.

As in our time, there was much fighting over land and power in Brother Lawrence's day, but he was unaffected by these concerns.

This is a play on words—in the French Old Testament, "the Lord" is usually translated as L'Eternel (the Eternal One).

Everything was the same to him—every place, every duty. The good brother found God everywhere, as much in repairing old, worn-out shoes as in praying with his community. He was not eager to go on spiritual retreats, because he found in his ordinary work the same God to love and to adore as in the depths of solitude.

Since his only means of going to God was to do everything out of love for Him, it did not matter to him what work he was given to do, provided that he did it for God. It was God, not the work, that he considered. He knew that the more such work crossed his natural inclinations, the more valuable was the love that made him offer it to God. He knew that the pettiness of the thing did not diminish in any way the value of his offering, because God, having need of nothing, considers only the love that accompanies our work.

Another characteristic of Brother Lawrence was his extraordinary firmness, which one would have called fearlessness in another kind of life. It revealed a noble soul that was raised above fear and above hope in anything except God. He admired nothing, was astonished by nothing, and feared nothing. His stability of soul came from the same source as all his other moral strengths. The lofty view he had of God made him think of Him, as He is in truth, as sovereign justice and infinite goodness. Trusting in this, he was assured that God would not deceive him, and that He would only do good to him, since he, on his part, was resolved never to displease Him and to do all and suffer all for His love.

I asked him one day who was his spiritual director. He answered that he had none, and that he did not think that he needed one, since the Rule and the duties he had in the religious life told him what he had to do outwardly, and the Gospel required him to love God with all his heart. Knowing that, a director seemed useless to him, but he added that he had great need of a confessor to remit his sins.

Those who conduct themselves in the spiritual life only by following their particular dispositions and feelings, who believe that they have nothing more important to do than to examine whether they are full of devotion or not—this sort of person could not possibly be stable or certain in his conduct, because these things change continually, whether by our own negligence, or by the order of God, who varies His gifts and His conduct towards us according to our needs.

The good brother, on the contrary, remained firm in the way of the faith that never changes. He was always the same, because he endeavored only to fulfill the duties of the place in which God had him, counting for merit only the virtues of his monastic state. Instead of paying attention to his feelings and continually examining the road on which he was walking, he looked at God, who is the end and purpose of the road, going with great strides toward Him by practicing righteousness, charity, and humility, and applying himself more to *doing* than to *thinking* about what he was doing.

The devotion of Brother Lawrence, built on this solid foundation, was not at all subject to visions or other extraordinary things. He was persuaded that even true visions are most often the marks of weakness in a soul that concentrates more on the gift than on God Himself. Outside of the period of his novitiate, he had nothing of this kind in his experience; at least he said nothing about visions to the people in whom he had the most confidence and to whom he opened his heart. He walked all his life in the footprints of the saints, by the sure path of faith. He never deviated from the ordinary road that leads to salvation by the exercises authorized for all time in the Church, by the practice of good works, and by the virtues of his monastic state. All other practices were suspect to him. His common sense and the light of his simple faith protected him from the reefs that so many souls encounter in their spiritual path. Many souls today are shipwrecked by giving themselves over to the love of novelty, to their own imaginations, to curiosity, and to human counsel.

Prepared by such a life, and following so sure a path, Brother Lawrence saw death approach without perturbance. His patience had been very great through the whole course of his life, but it increased even more as he approached death. He never seemed to have a moment of sorrow, even in the greatest violence of his illness. Joy appeared not only on his face, but also in the way he spoke, causing some brothers who went to visit him to ask if in fact he was not suffering at all.

"Forgive me," he told them. "I am suffering. This pleurisy in my side hurts me, but my spirit is at peace."

"But," they added, "if God wanted you to suffer these terrible pains for as long as ten years, would you be satisfied to do that?"

"I would," he said, "not only for that number of years, but if God wanted me to endure my ills until the Day of Judgment, I would willingly consent, and I would still hope that He would give me the grace to remain always content."

As the hour of his departure approached, he often exclaimed, "O Faith! Faith!"—expressing the excellence of his faith more in this way than if he had said more. He adored God without ceasing, and said to one Brother that he almost no longer *believed* in the presence of God in his soul, but by this luminous faith, he already *saw* something of God's intimate presence.

His courage was so great in a passage where all is to be feared that he said to one of his friends who questioned him about this point that he feared neither death nor hell, nor the judgment of God, nor the efforts of the devil.

Since his companions took pleasure in hearing him say such edifying things, they continued to ask him questions. They asked him if he knew that it is a terrible thing to fall into the hands of the living God, because no one knows assuredly whether he is worthy of love or hatred.

 This refers to Hebrews 10:31: "It is a fearful thing to fall into the hands of the living God."

"I agree," he said, "but I would not want to know, for I am afraid it would induce vanity in me. Nothing is better than to abandon ourselves to God."

After he had received the last sacraments, a brother asked him what he was doing, and what was going through his mind.

"I am doing what I will do throughout all eternity," he replied. "I am blessing God, I am praising God, and I am adoring and loving Him with all my heart. This sums up our entire call and duty, Brothers: to adore God and to love Him, without worrying about the rest."

These were the last sentiments of Brother Lawrence, who died soon afterward with the peace and tranquility in which he had lived. His death occurred on February 12, 1691, when he was about eighty years old.

Nothing better portrays a true Christian philosopher than what has just been related about the life and death of this good brother.

Here, Christian philosopher *is not used as a technical term, but as an ancient virtue of one who meets challenges with calmness and good humor.*

Such were those in times past who truly renounced the world to attend only to cultivating their souls and to knowing God and His Son Jesus Christ—men who took the Gospel as their rule and professed the holy wisdom of the Cross. This was the way St. Clement of Alexandria described them for us, and it seems that he had in mind a man like Brother Lawrence when he said that the principal duty of the philosopher, that is to say, the Christian sage, is prayer.

Clement of Alexandria was born around 150 and died around 216. He was known for combining Greek philosophy and Christian theology.

He prays in all places, not with many words, but in secret, in the depth of his soul. While walking, conversing, resting, reading or working, he continues to pray. He praises God continually, not only in the morning upon rising, and at noon, but in all his actions he gives glory to God like the seraphim of Isaiah. The close attention he gives to spiritual things through prayer makes him sweet, affable, patient, and, at the same time, severe even to the point of not being tempted. He allows neither pleasure nor pain to have any hold on him.

The joy of contemplation, upon which he continually eats his fill without being satiated with it, does not allow him to feel the little pleasures of earth. Through faith he already lives with the Lord, although his body still appears on earth; and after partaking through faith of God's inaccessible light, he has no more taste for the goods of this world. Through love he is already where he should be and desires nothing, because he has the object of his desire as far as it is possible to do so here on earth.

He has no need of becoming bold, because nothing in this life troubles him or is capable of turning him aside from the love of God. He has no need of becoming tranquil and never falls into becoming sad, because he is persuaded that all is well. He never becomes angry, and nothing stirs him up, because he always loves God and is entirely turned toward Him alone. He has no jealousy, because he lacks nothing. He loves no one with common friendship, but loves the Creator through His creatures.

His soul is steadfastly constant and is free from all change, since forgetting everything else, he is attached to God alone.

Although Brother Lawrence spent his life retired from the world in a monastery, there is still no one who cannot take great profit from what is given here concerning his way of life. He teaches people engaged in the world to turn to God, asking for grace as they fulfill their duties, take care of their business affairs, carry on conversations, and even engage in recreation. By his example they will be moved not only to give thanks to Him for His blessings and for the good His grace has allowed them to do, but also to humble themselves before Him for their faults.

This is not a speculative devotion that can be practiced only in monasteries. Every one of us must adore God and love Him, and no one can discharge these two great duties without linking with them a heart relationship that makes us depend on Him every moment, like children who have difficulty standing up without their mother at their side.

Not only is this not difficult, but it is easy and necessary for everyone. It is the very essence of the unceasing prayer that St. Paul commends to all Christians. Whoever does not do it is not aware of his needs or his incapacity to do anything good. He neither knows who he is nor who God is, nor the continual need he has of Jesus Christ.

The business and commerce of the world cannot serve as an excuse for neglecting our duty. God is everywhere. We can speak to Him no matter where we are. Our hearts can speak to Him in a thousand different ways. All we need is a little love, and then living this way will not be difficult.

Those who live in monastic communities, removed from the commotion of the world, have still more to gain from Brother Lawrence's way of life. Since they are freed from most of the needs and proprieties that burden those who are engaged in worldly affairs, there is nothing to prevent them from following the example of this good brother in rejecting any thought other than of doing all their actions for the love of God, and giving Him, as he says, all for all. Brother Lawrence's general detachment from the world, his total forgetfulness of himself, which he carried as far as not thinking about his own salvation in order to occupy himself solely with God, his indifference to the types of duties or assignments he was given, and his freedom in spiritual exercises—all these should be a very helpful example to them as they seek to live their lives for God.

Study Guide

Brother Lawrence's *Practicing the Presence of God* has long been touted as an "everyman's" guide to spirituality. After reading this, do you think he is really as simple as his biographers portray him?

Which parts of his practice of life most appeal to you?

Which parts of his practice do you consider too difficult to incorporate into your life?

Brother Lawrence was of course a monk, and chances are, you are not. But how might his way of life be adapted for those of us who are not?

What would you have to change in your life to become more like Brother Lawrence?

What would you not want to change?

He implies that he left the common practices—worship, confession of sin, prayers—behind at a certain point in his life and instead simply dwelt with God. Do agree with Brother Lawrence that these practices are really just media to get to the real essence of spirituality, which is unity with God?

Brother Lawrence was not a typical monk. Monastic spirituality is idealized in ways that lead us to think that all monks are like Brother Lawrence. How do you suppose his fellow monks felt about his life with God?

If you had the chance to converse with Brother Lawrence, what would you ask him?

What do you think he would ask you?

About Paraclete Press

Who We Are

Paraclete Press is a publisher of books, recordings, and DVDs on Christian spirituality. Our publishing represents a full expression of Christian belief and practice—from Catholic to Evangelical, from Protestant to Orthodox.

We are the publishing arm of the Community of Jesus, an ecumenical monastic community in the Benedictine tradition. As such, we are uniquely positioned in the marketplace without connection to a large corporation and with informal relationships to many branches and denominations of faith.

What We Are Doing

Books

Paraclete publishes books that show the richness and depth of what it means to be Christian. Although Benedictine spirituality is at the heart of all that we do, we publish books that reflect the Christian experience across many cultures, time periods, and houses of worship. We publish books that nourish the vibrant life of the church and its people—books about spiritual practice, formation, history, ideas, and customs.

We have several different series, including the best-selling Living Library, Paraclete Essentials, and Paraclete Giants series of classic texts in contemporary English; A Voice from the Monastery—men and women monastics writing about living a spiritual life today; award-winning literary faith fiction and poetry; and the Active Prayer Series that brings creativity and liveliness to any life of prayer.

Recordings

From Gregorian chant to contemporary American choral works, our music recordings celebrate sacred choral music through the centuries. Paraclete distributes the recordings of the internationally acclaimed choir Gloriæ Dei Cantores, praised for their "rapt and fathomless spiritual intensity" by *American Record Guide*, and the Gloriæ Dei Cantores Schola, which specializes in the study and performance of Gregorian chant. Paraclete is also the exclusive North American distributor of the recordings of the Monastic Choir of St. Peter's Abbey in Solesmes, France, long considered to be a leading authority on Gregorian chant.

DVDs

Our DVDs offer spiritual help, healing and biblical guidance for life issues: grief and loss, marriage, forgiveness, anger management, facing death, and spiritual formation.

Learn more about us at our Web site:
www.paracletepress.com,
or call us toll-free at 1-800-451-5006.

Also from Tony Jones:

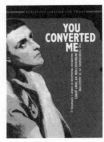

You Converted Me
The Confessions of St. Augustine
Introduction and Notes by Tony Jones
Modernized Translation by Robert J. Edmonson, CJ
ISBN: 978-1-55725-463-4
232 pages
$16.95, Trade paper

"A boy grows into a man, getting into the kind of mischief that a lot of boys do (messing around with girls, stealing, getting in trouble at school). Meanwhile, his over-protective Christian mother prays fervently for the salvation of his soul. . . ."

> "*You Converted Me* makes Augustine's classic Confessions
> accessible and available to readers today–young or old,
> religious or not." —Brian McLaren, author/activist

The Most Difficult Journey You'll Ever Make
The Pilgrim's Progress
Introduction and Notes by Tony Jones
Modernized Translation by Robert J. Edmonson, CJ
ISBN: 978-1-55725-464-1
241 pages
$14.95, Trade paper

The Pilgrim's Progress is a frank depiction of the Christian life. Written by an imprisoned pastor almost 350 years ago, it still captures attention with its vivid depictions of the journey of an ordinary Christian . . .

> "A terrific modernized version of a classic."
> —Will Penner, youth pastor, speaker,
> Executive Editor of *The Journal of Student Ministries*

Available from most booksellers or through Paraclete Press
www.paracletepress.com • 1-800-451-5006
Try your local bookstore first.

Other Christian Classics from Paraclete...

The Imitation of Christ
Thomas à Kempis
ISBN: 978-0941478-07-6
252 pages, Trade paper, $12.95

The Imitation of Christ has enjoyed an unparalleled place in the world of books for more than five hundred years, second only to the Bible itself. A manual of devotion to God, this classic continues to change the lives of people of all backgrounds and denominations.

Meditations on the Heart of God
François Fénelon
ISBN: 978-1-55725-181-7
170 pages, Trade paper, $14.95

For three centuries, men and women have found consolation in the wisdom and counsel of François Fénelon. This modern translation focuses on how to seek God in the midst of the affairs of everyday life. Fénelon's words will comfort and encourage all who desire to know God.

The Cloud of Unknowing
Anonymous
ISBN: 978-1-55725-445-0
114 pages, Trade paper, $11.95

Written by an anonymous fourteenth-century author, *The Cloud of Unknowing* was originally prepared for cloistered monks. Yet this little book has blessed centuries of readers from all walks of life. Each brief chapter offers a way to enter into the life of prayer and provides common sense steps on this mystical path.

The Story of a Soul
St. Thérèse of Lisieux
ISBN: 978-1-55725-487-0
300 pages
Trade paper, $16.95

Thérèse of Lisieux's desire was not to be mighty and great, but to be a humble little flower that would gladden God's eyes. Canonized in 1925, she was declared a Doctor of the Church in 1997 by Pope John Paul II.

Available from most booksellers or through Paraclete Press
www.paracletepress.com • 1-800-451-5006
Try your local bookstore first.